- What *is* continuing education — have we agreed on its definition and purpose?
- How does educating adults differ from educating traditional college students?
- Why have administrators and practitioners been hesitant to address some of the problems in continuing education?

Here is a timely, thought-provoking book that deals with the crucial questions that face continuing educators today. Pointing out that most continuing educators do not have the luxury of extra time, the author argues that the future of continuing education requires that everyone concerned with the development of the field *take* the time to identify and analyze the problems still to be overcome.

The book begins with an analysis of the problems related to characteristics of the human species, then moves on to discuss problems related to the characteristics of adults as learners, problems related to the *context* of continuing education, problems related to *program planning,* to *teaching and learning,* and to *research* in continuing education. The author challenges many accepted beliefs about the definition, purpose, and planning of continuing education, while presenting alternative views about each problem discussed. A special section on *how to analyze problems* helps stimulate the reader's own analysis of the problems and issues raised.

**THE McGRAW-HILL SERIES IN THE
MANAGEMENT AND ADMINISTRATION
OF CONTINUING EDUCATION**

Consulting Editor:
Rosalind K. Loring, Dean
College of Continuing Education
University of Southern California

Apps PROBLEMS IN CONTINUING EDUCATION

Cooper ETHICS FOR EDUCATING THE LIFELONG LEARNER

Farlow PUBLICIZING AND PROMOTING PROGRAMS

Lenz CREATIVE PROGRAMMING AND MARKETING IN CONTINUING EDUCATION

PROBLEMS IN
CONTINUING
EDUCATION

Jerold W. Apps

Professor of Continuing Education
Chairman, Department of Continuing and Vocational Education
University of Wisconsin—Madison

McGRAW-HILL BOOK COMPANY

New York   St. Louis   San Francisco   Auckland   Bogotá   Düsseldorf   Johannesburg
London   Madrid   Mexico   Montreal   New Delhi   Panama   Paris   São Paulo
Singapore   Sydney   Tokyo   Toronto

Library of Congress Cataloging in Publication Data

Apps, Jerold W   date
    Problems in continuing education.

    (The McGraw-Hill series in the management and
administration of continuing education)
    Includes Index.
    1. Adult education—United States. 2. Continuing
education—United States. I. Title. II. Series.
LC5251.A87   374.9'73   79-11256
ISBN 0-07-002159-7

PROBLEMS IN CONTINUING EDUCATION

1 2 3 4 5 6 7 8 9 0 DODO 7 8 3 2 1 0 9

This book was set in Helvetica by Black Dot, Inc.
The editors were Robert G. Manley and Edwin Hanson;
the designer was Anne Canevari Green;
the production supervisor was Richard A. Ausburn.
R. R. Donnelley & Sons Company was printer and binder.

CONTENTS

ACKNOWLEDGMENTS

I am indebted to many people for the preparation of this book. I am particularly grateful to the graduate students who have worked with me over the years and helped me to put into focus many of the problems discussed on these pages.

I want to thank Professor Joan Wright, North Carolina State University at Raleigh; Dr. M. Donald Campbell, University of Illinois; and Arthur Lloyd, Basic Choices, Madison, Wisconsin, for reading and critically evaluating the manuscript.

Others who read sections of the manuscript and offered critical comment include Professor Patrick Boyle, Dr. Ronald Jimmerson, John Fiss, and Joe Donaldson, all with the University of Wisconsin—Madison.

I particularly want to thank Gloria Hay and Mary Marshall, who helped greatly to put the manuscript into final form. Nancy Trager receives my special thanks for typing the various drafts of the manuscript.

And to my wife, Ruth, and children, Susan, Steve, and Jeff, I owe thanks for final preparation of the book—proofreading has become a family project.

Lastly, to Robert Manley, my editor at McGraw-Hill, I owe sincere thanks for his encouragement and his patience.

Jerold W. Apps

PROBLEMS IN
CONTINUING EDUCATION

SECTION I

OVERVIEW

F ew of us have been able to enjoy the luxury of taking time out from planning, promoting, teaching, evaluating, and administering continuing education programs in order to reflect upon our work. Yet it will be argued throughout this book that if the theory *and* practice of continuing education is to advance, we must all take time out to identify and wrestle with the problems of the field.

To tackle this project of examining problems in continuing education, we have divided this book into sections of two or three chapters each. In this overview section, we describe the rationale, structure, and contents of the book.

Chapter 1 includes a description of the background of the book and a discussion of why it is important to consider problems basic to the field of continuing education.

Chapter 2 includes a definition of the word "problem," a discussion of various dimensions of problems, and a description of the difference between convergent and divergent problems. Also included in this chapter are several reasons why many educators of adults are reluctant to tackle basic problems.

CHAPTER 1

Introduction

Many a night, at a conference or workshop, my peers in continuing education and I huddled around tables and talked about such problems as inadequate budgets, unreasonable requests for reports, adult participation that was clearly less than anticipated, and teaching approaches that did not work. Never was there a shortage of problems for us to discuss.

After several years of experience and many discussions about problems, I saw little evidence that they were being resolved. In fact, each year spawned a new set of problems in addition to those that remained unresolved.

Soon it became obvious that there were many more problems than I and my peers, all working together, could ever reasonably hope to resolve. So we resorted to working on those problems that forced their attention on us. We put out brush fires as they erupted. This strategy, of course, left the many other problems smoldering in the background, like an endangered forest that had not yet burst into flame.

As I reflected on this dilemma, it occurred to me that not all problems were at the same level. Some were more basic than others. Slowly I began to realize that perhaps we could make more progress in solving everyday problems like budgeting and the promotion of programs if we spent more time attending to these basic problems.

It is in these basic problems that all everyday "practical" problems have their roots. By analyzing basic problems, we become more effective. When we analyze a basic problem, we are in turn touching on a whole array of practical problems that the educators of adults face. For instance, let's say your question is how to plan an educational program for fifty adults active in a senior citizen center. Anyone who has tried to do this knows that it involves many practical considerations. These can be traced back to such basic questions as: Who should plan educational programs? What should be the purpose of continuing education programs? Is there a difference between an educational program and a noneducational program?

Several years ago, when I began teaching a course on the philosophy of continuing education, it became clear to me that many people were interested in exploring what I call the more basic problems of the field. Based on those first years of teaching, I wrote a monograph related to the topic of my course.[1] In that monograph, I presented a framework for developing one's own working philosophy of adult continuing education. In many ways *Problems in Continuing Education* builds on this earlier work with more in-depth discussion. Also, many problem areas not included in the monograph are presented in this volume.

THE NATURE OF THIS BOOK

Before saying more about what this book is, let's look at what it is not. It is not a historical analysis of the field of continuing education, though occasionally we will look at the historical roots of a problem.

This book is not a descriptive one. It does not describe continuing education programs and activities, although examples will be used freely when a given problem area is discussed and examples seem relevant.

This book is not a research report in the traditional sense of defining a research problem and collecting, summarizing, and drawing conclusions about data. Neither is this a how-to-do-it book. A number of excellent books in the field of continuing education have been written for the practitioner who needs how-to-do-it information about planning programs, teaching effectively, and evaluating efforts.

What, then, is this book? What is its purpose? And what is its focus? The concern is with basic problems in continuing education. For instance, we consider problems associated with understanding human nature, defining who is an adult, the definition and purpose of continuing education, planning and teaching, and research in continuing education.

Though this is not a traditional research book, it can be described as a kind of research in progress, for it attempts to define, analyze, and in some

[1] Jerold W. Apps, *Toward a Working Philosophy of Adult Education*, Syracuse University, Syracuse, N.Y., 1973.

instances offer solutions to the fundamental problems identified. To do this, I draw on empirical research reports, history, philosophical writings, and—of course—my own experience.

Rather than isolate problems from the context in which they occur, I will look at the broader picture. I will be concerned with how the problem we are examining relates to other problems. For instance, the way in which we answer the question about human nature relates to questions about teaching and learning, the purposes of agencies and institutions of continuing education, and research approaches.

My premise is that to look intelligently at any basic problem we must constantly keep in mind the complete picture—the totality of continuing education. Rather than isolate a problem from its context, we undergird our work here with the assumption that the totality of the field of continuing education is more than the sum of its parts. Thus, I argue that it is impossible to deal with any of the problems of the field without keeping in mind the totality—that is, the context in which the problems occur and the relations between problems. But, on the other hand, it is possible to examine problems by themselves provided that we always remember and keep in focus their relationship to the entire field and to each other.

A practical example of what I am talking about is the malfunctioning of some of our technology, as in the Bay Area Rapid Transit (BART). In writing about BART's problems, Rasa Gustaitis tells of doors opening while trains were moving and trains racing past stations without stopping. The problem, Gustaitis says, is that the designers of BART, and of many other malfunctioning inventions, concentrated on isolated design problems without first focusing on a conception of the finished product. Those creations that have been successful were first a picture—a vision—in the minds of those who created them. The totality came first, then the work on the parts.[2]

THE STRUCTURE OF THIS BOOK

This book is divided into sections, and each section is divided into chapters. Each section is designed to deal with one basic problem area. Within the section chapters, I have done three things: (1) identified a basic problem, usually by raising questions; (2) looked at the problem from several perspectives, sometimes comparing and contrasting divergent solutions to the problem; (3) selected either a suggested solution to the problem or offered guidelines for developing a solution or a perspective for the problem.

You, the reader, may or may not wish to accept the suggested solution or

[2]Rasa Gustaitis, "Over-reliance on Machines May Explain Why Things Fail," *The Capital Times*, Madison, Wis., Sept. 30, 1977.

proposed guidelines for developing a solution or a perspective. That is, upon studying the analysis of the problem as presented here, you may reach a different conclusion. It is not so important that you accept the suggested solutions or guidelines as it is that you wrestle with the problem and do your own analyzing and searching for solutions and perspectives. This book is designed to assist in this process of searching, analyzing, and making decisions about basic problems.

Some of the material may be familiar. I have included information about program planning, information about teaching–learning theories, and the like. I considered excluding this information and simply referring the reader to other sources, but since many readers will not have easy access to the sources quoted here, I have retained this material.

Understand, though, that the material on such matters as teaching–learning theories and program planning approaches is included as a way of clarifying various perspectives on a problem area. As I said earlier, this is not a how-to-do-it book but a *problems* book. I am concerned about identifying, analyzing, and offering some tentative conclusions and perspectives about basic problems in the field of continuing education.

Section II is concerned with those who participate in continuing education. Chapter 3 raises questions about human nature and suggests several alternative positions. Chapter 4 opens up the question of how we characterize adults.

Section III takes us into a discussion of the context of the field of continuing education. Chapter 5 raises questions about how we describe the field. In Chapter 6, we explore the question of what the purpose(s) of continuing education should be. Chapter 7 presents guidelines for developing an answer to the question of the purpose of continuing education.

Section IV explores the question of the content of continuing education. Chapter 8 focuses on various viewpoints of knowledge. Chapter 9 identifies problems with planning approaches, and Chapter 10 presents guidelines for new approaches to curriculum development in continuing education.

Section V deals with procedures for continuing education, or with questions of means and methods. In Chapter 11, I identify several problems concerning procedures, and in Chapter 12, the topic of developing a teaching–learning rationale is discussed.

Finally, in Section VI, the problems of research in continuing education are explored. Chapter 13 presents some of these problems, while Chapter 14 offers guidelines for developing alternative approaches to research in continuing education.

CHAPTER 2

A Perspective on Problems

Before we begin looking at specific problems in continuing education, let's look at a difficulty with the concept of *problem*. What do we mean by the word? Can we learn more about the ways in which we define and use problems, so that we'll be able to deal with them more effectively?

"PROBLEM" DEFINED

By "problem" we mean *questions(s) raised for inquiry, for solution, or for both*.

There are three components to this definition. First, problems are questions. Second, they are questions that may be raised *either* for inquiry *or* for solution. Third, they are questions that may be raised for *both* inquiry and solution.

When a question is raised for the purpose of solving a problem, the focus is on answering the question (solving the problem). When a question is raised for inquiry about a problem, the person asking the question is interested in the problem itself, the component parts of the problem, the effect of this problem on other problems, the location of the problem, and perhaps something about the history of the problem.

Thus it is possible for us to consider and work on problems at levels that do not always involve attempting to solve them. Indeed, as we shall argue later in this chapter, some problems facing continuing education cannot be solved. But this doesn't mean they shouldn't be dealt with.

Let us take the definition of "problem" and turn it back on itself. In other words, what questions can we ask about the concept *problem* itself? In what ways is this concept a problem for us?

Let us begin by asking two questions: What are the dimensions of problems and what are the barriers that prevent those in continuing education from inquiring about and/or attempting to solve the problems they face? The rest of this chapter will be devoted to these two questions.

DIMENSIONS OF PROBLEMS

Let us consider three dimensions of a problem: (1) how a problem relates to science and philosophy, (2) the problem's time perspective, and (3) the extent to which the problem is solvable or not.

Relationship to Science and Philosophy

For our purposes, there are two broad categories of questions: scientific questions and philosophic questions. That is, in relation to continuing education, we can distinguish those questions which relate to continuing education as a "science" and those which emerge from our philosophy of education.

By scientific questions we mean questions whose answers are subject to careful checking and verification. A scientific question usually deals with an area where the dimensions of the questions can be carefully controlled and measured. The following are examples of scientific questions within continuing education: What instructional approaches will provide the greatest gain in knowledge when history is being taught to a group of adults? What is the effect of an adult's age on the ability to learn? What is the relationship of previous formal study in liberal education to participation in continuing education programs?

Philosophic questions deal with areas where the dimensions of the question cannot be tightly controlled and where the answers are not susceptible to empirical test and/or measurement. Thus philosophic questions are often broader and more pervasive than scientific questions. While the answers to scientific questions enjoy rather widespread acceptance (assuming procedures were done carefully and properly), the answers to philosophic questions, which almost always relate to fundamental values, are often hotly debated and seldom agreed upon.[1]

[1]See John S. Brubacher, *Modern Philosophies of Education*, 3d ed., McGraw-Hill, New York, 1962, for an expanded discussion of the difference between science and philosophy in relation to education.

Examples of philosophic questions in continuing education include the following: What should be the purposes of continuing education? How do educators deal with conflicting values in any continuing education activity?

The basic differences between scientific and philosophic questions lie in three broad areas: (1) primary concerns, (2) procedures for seeking answers, and (3) the nature of the answer obtained.

Primary Concerns   Scientific questions, as suggested above, deal with those matters that can be carefully controlled. This usually means a well-defined and precise approach to problem situations. In order to deal with a problem in depth, the scientist looks at specific questions related to the problem and proceeds to seek answers to these specific questions.

The scientist asks three kinds of questions: (1) descriptive, (2) explanatory, and (3) predictive. Descriptive questions help us understand the characteristics of a phenomenon. For example, a descriptive question could be: What are the characteristics of people who enroll in a great books program?

Explanatory questions help us explain the occurrence of a phenomenon. An example of an explanatory question is: Why do people enroll in a great books program?

Predictive questions help us predict the occurrence of a phenomenon. For example, if factors *a* and *b* exist, then we can predict, with a certain level of probability, that phenomenon *c* will occur. Or, to put the example in question form: What factors affect people's participation in a great books program?

Philosophic questions are those related to metaphysics, epistemology, and axiology. Metaphysics is the study of reality and attempts to answer the broad question: What is? Someone dealing with metaphysics might, for example, ask: How does one distinguish between appearances and what actually is? In a more practical way, adult educators are raising metaphysical questions when they ask: What is the nature of the adult learner? Are adults essentially directed from within, or are they directed by some balance between inner and outer forces? How much freedom do individuals have to make decisions and what, in fact, do we mean by freedom? What is the nature of society? What is the nature of continuing education agencies and institutions? What is the relationship of adult learners or teachers to the society in which they live? What is the relationship of the adult learner to the natural environment?

Epistemology is concerned with knowledge and asks: How do we know? What is knowledge and what are the sources of knowledge are questions of epistemology. Educators of adults are vitally concerned with epistemological questions. These educators ask: What is knowledge from the perspective of the adult learner and from the perspective of the educator? Is knowledge only that which results from scientific endeavors? Can knowledge come from within the learner? What is the difference between learning and knowing? What is the relation of learning to knowing?

Axiology, the third field of philosophy, is concerned with theories of value and ethics—what is good and what is bad, what is right and what is wrong. Examples of axiological questions include the following: With whom should educators of adults work? How should educators relate to conflicting social groups? What purposes should continuing education programs seek to attain? What is the relationship of the educator's values to the values of the people with whom he or she works? What is the place of values and ethics in continuing education programming? And, to be more precise, whose values are incorporated in continuing education programs?

Many philosophical questions are of a normative nature; that is, they raise the "should-be" question. These should-be questions get at the standards for the field, help educators of adults focus on their basic commitments, and help those in the field of continuing education to determine their direction.

Procedures for Obtaining Answers Answers to scientific questions are obtained through procedures commonly referred to as the scientific method. Philosophic questions are answered through a process of systematic reflection. See Chapters 13 and 14 for a discussion of research approaches in continuing education.

The Nature of the Answer Obtained In the field of continuing education, the answer to a scientific question is one that can be verified through observation or through experimentation; it can often be expressed in quantifiable terms. Thus the answer to a scientific question is usually more precise than the answer to a philosophic question. The philosophic answer often includes both quantifiable information and nonquantifiable material.

Answers to philosophic questions are frequently not susceptible to verification for two primary reasons: they are usually more comprehensive than answers to scientific questions and they always are based upon or include implicit (or explicit) value judgments. Philosophic answers are often more comprehensive than empirical answers because they may draw on such disciplines as psychology, history, sociology, physiology, genetics, and social work as well as from the disciplines of anthropology, geriatrics, and political science—that is, from social or behavioral sciences that often do not lend themselves to precise measurement. Philosophic answers may also include material from such arts as poetry, drama, and fiction.

A philosophic response to a question may draw from the experiences of educators of adults and adult learners. Because experience is integral, it often cannot be categorized neatly by discipline or measure.

The answers to philosophic questions always have normative implications. That is, they presuppose standards for the directions that continuing education should take and the practice that should be followed in the field. Such statements as, "Continuing education should (or should not) be involved in social change" and "Adults should be involved in making decisions about what they wish to learn" are examples of normative statements pertinent to the field.

Because answers to philosophic questions often draw from a wide spectrum of disciplines and experience and because philosophic answers always include a normative dimension, there is often disagreement concerning the answers. Scientific answers, on the other hand, are usually more limited in scope and, because they deal with dimensions that are more carefully controlled, answers to such questions are more apt to be agreed upon.

Relationships among Questions So far we have attempted to show how scientific and philosophic questions are different from each other. But because they are different doesn't mean they are not related.

One relationship, and an important one, is that asking a philosophic question and working at answering it often results in the raising of several scientific questions. And, conversely, the process of asking and seeking for answers to scientific questions often spawns many philosophic questions.

For example, the exploration of the philosophic question "What should be the purposes of adult education?" may suggest the scientific question "What purposes do cooperative extension agents see for adult education?"

And, conversely, if we start with the scientific question "What purposes do cooperative extension agents see for adult education?" we might be prompted to ask the broader philosophic question "What should be the purposes of adult education?" Thus one type of question often suggests additional questions of the other type.

Let's look at an example outside of education, in the area of transportation. A philosophic question might be "What should be the means by which people are transported from one place to another?" Scientific questions growing out of that question might be "Which is more economical, riding a city bus to work or riding in a car pool?" "Which mode of transportation is least polluting, the passenger train or the airplane?" The philosophic question clearly relates to the scientific questions, but one type of question does not subsume the other. By answering the scientific questions, we have not answered the philosophic question. And, obviously, by answering the philosophic question, we have not answered the scientific questions.

Let's take the example a bit further. To answer the question "What should be the means by which people are transported?" we might poll various interested groups and ask them. Let's say the results of our poll show that 74 percent of the people polled believe that personally owned automobiles should continue to be the primary mode of transportation. Does this give us the answer to our philosophic question "What should be the means by which people are transported from one place to another?" No, it does not. What we have is the summary of what those who were polled believe should be the primary mode of transportation. That is, we have the answer to the scientific question "What does a sample of people believe should be the primary mode of transportation?" The philosophic question still remains unanswered. It cannot be answered simply by polling people, although the poll information may contribute to the philosophic answer.

In summary then, scientific and philosophic questions, though clearly different from each other, are often related. Both types of questions are necessary to deal with most problem areas. Philosophic questions deal with basic judgments and values for which there are no *right* answers. On the other hand, scientific questions are those for which we can supply quantifiable answers by agreed-upon methods.

Perhaps we might say that science helps us deal with what is while philosophy raises questions about the meaning of what is and about what should be. These two sets of questions are in tension. *What is* is not a given when we are dealing with human beings in society. On the other hand, *what should be* cannot be abstracted from the way people are and how they have jointly organized their lives.

We must also avoid the trap of believing that one type of question is better than the other. Science has given us much, but it cannot begin to answer all the questions—particularly those that directly involve value judgments about human beings. Likewise, it would be naïve to suggest that philosophy has all the answers. Our position here is that science deals with a different set of questions than does philosophy, and both sets of questions must be asked. By asking both sets of questions about a given problem area, we improve our chances of obtaining answers that are comprehensive and useful.

A Problem's Time Perspective

Besides having a scientific or philosophic dimension to them, problems also have a time dimension. As we attempt to analyze a problem, we must determine whether it relates to the past, the present, or the future.

On the surface, this sounds surprisingly simple. But too often, because the time dimension is not considered when someone attempts to deal with a problem, confusion results. For instance, let's say the problem that we want to learn more about concerns the content of adult learning. We can look at this broad area from several perspectives. We can ask questions like: What have adults learned in the past? What are adults learning now? What will adults probably be learning in the future? What *should* adults be learning in the future?

As you might imagine, our approach to inquiring about and attempting to solve problems will depend to some extent on whether we are dealing with the past, the present, or the future.

Often, as we attempt to learn more about a problem, we combine several of these time dimensions. That is, we try to learn as much as we can about the history of the problem and about the present situation; then, based on that information, we attempt to predict what the future situation will probably be or ought to be.

In this process, we seem to have the most difficulty distinguishing between the predicted future and the ideal future. Or, to put it another way, we have difficulty separating what is likely to happen—based on what is presently happening and what has happened in the past—from what (we think) *should* happen in the future. Many writers and researchers refuse to consider the should-be question because their scientific approaches will, at best, give them only supporting data—and often not even that. Scientific research approaches will not provide the answers to the questions of what should be. As we pointed out in the preceding section, these are philosophic questions which can be answered only through philosophical research and a clarification of the values we espouse.

Solvable and Insolvable Problems

The common attitude in the Western world is that eventually we will be able to solve all our problems. We reason that what prevents us from solving every problem is a lack of resources—either material or human—or a lack of know-how. Given the necessary time and resources, we believe, we will eventually develop the know-how to solve any problem. Few consider the possibility that some problems may be inherently insolvable and should be recognized as such.

E. F. Schumacher[2] challenges the position that every problem has a possible solution. He argues, first, that there are most definitely problems that are insolvable, and that, second, the very existence of insolvable problems is itself a positive thing. Let's look at Schumacher's position and then see how it applies to continuing education.

Schumacher talks about convergent and divergent problems. Convergent problems have the potential for being solved. Divergent problems are insolvable.

Convergent Problems As people work on a convergent problem, take it apart, look at its components, and search out data that relate to it, they find that the more they work on it, the more their answers begin to come together or

[2]E. F. Schumacher, *A Guide for the Perplexed*, Harper & Row, New York, 1977.

converge. They find all paths beginning to lead to the same destination—that is, the solution to the problem or the answer to the question they have asked.

The classical problem-solving method provides a process by which we may deal with and attempt to solve convergent problems.

Basically there are two types of convergent problems: (1) those that can be solved immediately or in the near future and (2) those that we know have the potential for being solved but remain unsolved because we may not yet have the technology or necessary resources for solving them. In other instances, priorities may have shifted so that the problem is no longer being given much attention.

An example of a convergent problem (solvable but not yet solved) relates to space travel. With a high priority allotted to space travel—in terms of both monetary and human resources—this country could place a manned space station in orbit within a few years. The problem is potentially solvable, though it has not been solved as yet.

Divergent Problems   When the responses to a question diverge or separate rather than converge or come together, we have what Schumacher calls a divergent problem. When we and others work on a divergent problem, we often discover answers that, though plausible and supportable, are contradictory to each other. The more we work on the problem, the more it becomes clear that we cannot all agree on a single answer or solution.

For example, within the field of continuing education, the question of how adult learning is facilitated is a divergent problem. At the present time, there are two major opposing answers to that question. On the one hand, there are the behaviorists, represented by B. F. Skinner, who say that learning is facilitated by reducing wholes to pieces and *learning* each piece. When the *learnings* of the pieces are added together, we will have an understanding of the whole.

On the other hand, there are the gestalt–field theorists who claim that learning is facilitated when we learn wholes as wholes, and that the whole or gestalt is more than the sum of its parts. Thus we cannot take situations apart and concentrate on the pieces in isolation from each other with any hope of understanding the whole. We must always look at the subsections of a whole in relation to one another and to the whole itself.

Those who are searching for single answers to problems will immediately ask, "Which is correct? Are the behaviorists right about how adult learning is facilitated, or are the gestalt–field theorists right?" What too often happens is that educators—after some thinking, reading, and perhaps formal study emphasizing one position or the other—take sides. They become behaviorists in their orientation, or they become gestalt–field advocates. Of course, this does not solve the original problem of how adult learning is facilitated, though it may satisfy those who believe that single solutions are necessary. But as long as there is an apparently viable alternative solution, the problem is not solved.

As more people work on the problem of how adult learning can be facilitated, the answers become increasingly divergent. And many educators of adults will become increasingly frustrated as they find themselves being forced to take sides.

Until we come to realize that this problem is insolvable, we will not be able to deal with it intelligently. The two basic approaches—gestalt–field and behaviorist—reflect two differing views as to how people learn, and considerable evidence can be mustered for each. The difficulties lie in the assumptions that educators bring to each of these situations. Those who subscribe to behaviorism have a different set of assumptions about the nature of human beings than those who advocate the gestalt–field approach to learning. (See Chapter 12 for a discussion of these assumptions.) As long as we continue to seek single answers to insolvable problems, we will continue to face frustration. That is, we will either fail to find answers or be forced to take sides, constantly defending the adequacy of our views against the opposition.

The fact that a problem is insolvable does not excuse us from dealing with it. The training that most of us received in our formal schooling emphasized finding a single solution to a problem. We learned that if we could not find a single solution, we should set the problem aside as either irrelevant or one which we did not have the resources to solve. This, of course, confused the issue. We did not learn how to separate the problem that was insolvable in the short run but potentially solvable in time from the problem that was inherently insolvable.

Dealing with Insolvable Problems   If, by definition, we cannot solve the insolvable problem and if it makes no sense to simply toss it aside as irrelevant, what do we do with it? To begin, we clearly need to determine whether the problem actually is a divergent or insolvable problem. What criteria can we use to identify such problems?

There are two general criteria that can help us separate convergent from divergent problems. Schumacher says, "convergence may be expected with regard to any problem which does not involve life, consciousness, self-awareness, which means [we are more likely to find convergence] in the fields of physics, chemistry, astronomy, and also in the abstract spheres like geometry and mathematics, or games like chess."[3] When, on the other hand, we begin dealing with those problems that are purely of a human nature, then we must expect a considerable amount of divergence. In sum, then, we can

[3]Ibid., p. 125.

expect to find solvable problems largely in the nonhuman areas. When we are dealing with human beings, on the other hand, particularly with their growth and learning, we can expect to find many insolvable problems.

Another way to recognize whether a problem is convergent or divergent is to begin working on it. If, as we work on the problem, we find that the answers increasingly come together until we can write down a single answer to our problem, the problem is a convergent problem. And if we find that the answers are moving further and further apart, we probably have a divergent problem.

Once we have recognized that we are dealing with an insolvable problem, what do we do? As suggested above, we should tackle insolvable problems and consider them worthy of our time and effort even as we recognize that no final answer is possible. Indeed, for educators of adults, the insolvable problem is often the most important problem to be dealt with.

What approaches do we follow, then?

1. We learn as much as we can about the problem. We work on it from every angle. We clearly determine that the problem is a divergent, insolvable problem. We examine the alternative solutions that occur to us. We try to avoid taking sides while also acquainting ourselves with opposing positions and their implications or consequences.

2. Once we clearly know we are dealing with an insolvable problem, we figure out ways of *transcending* the problem. That is, we seek ways of applying all the alternative solutions to the problem rather than accepting one of the alternatives—that is, taking sides. Let us, for example, go back to the problem of facilitating learning for adults. If we agree that it has no single solution, what can we do to take advantage of both solutions—the behaviorist and the gestalt–field approaches? Can we imagine working with adults at the same time or in the same situation with both approaches in mind? Are we able to set aside years of training that suggest the need for single answers, even when we face a question that has two or more opposing answers?

   Using the example of learning approaches, can we facilitate our students' learning by providing what might be called behavioristic experiences at some times and what might be called gestalt–field experiences at others?

So far we have talked about how we might adjust to an insolvable problem. I do not want to leave the impression that all we must do is learn how to adjust to such problems. The concept of insolvable problems is more important than that.

We must openly search for the insolvable problem as well as attempt to identify and define the solvable one. Because the insolvable problem often has solutions that are in opposition to each other, the insolvable problem involves a certain tension. For many people, tension is a condition that we should either seek to eliminate or try to avoid. Here I am using the word in a positive sense. Because a tension exists in an insolvable problem, our sensitivity to the problem is heightened, our concern for the problem is continuing, and our eagerness to respond to the problem is increased.

For example, let's say the problem we are facing is whether or not a continuing education program should remain the same or be changed. Members of our planning committee argue strongly that the program should continue as it has existed in the past. They point out the successes of the program. They provide evidence from the evaluations of previous students that the program has indeed been successful. There is every reason to believe that the program will be equally successful in the future. But there is another group, just as vocal, that points out the large number of people who might be involved in the program but are not. If the program were changed, this large group of people might also take part.

If we try to force a single answer to the question raised, we will find ourselves joining one or the other of the two groups who support divergent positions on the question.

But if we attempt to transcend the problem and recognize the healthy tension that exists between those who support stability and those who support change, we will be able to build a stronger program than we would if we decided on one or the other of the single solutions.

Of course, the issues we are discussing go far beyond continuing education. The problem of stability versus change is one that has faced humanity throughout the ages. Some have always argued that things should remain as they are while others have insisted on the importance of change.

In short, there has always been a healthy tension between those who want stability and those who want change. I would argue that this is as it should be. It is for us to find ways to encourage this healthy tension to continue and to transcend problems of this type.

Paulo Freire, an adult educator who has specialized in literacy education, looks at the insolvable problem in ways which complement what we have said above. Arthur Lloyd, in his analysis of Freire's concept of *problematization*, writes as follows:

Problematization is, in Freire's use, distinct from "problem-solving". . . . *Problem-solving suggests the analysis of a problem by experts, the identification of component parts, the devising of means of resolving difficulties in the most efficient way, and on this basis the development of a strategy for solving the problem. Viewed in this manner problem-solving distorts the totality of human experience by reducing it to those dimensions susceptible to treatment as mere difficulties to be resolved.*

By problematization, on the other hand, Freire suggests a process by which a people can "decodify" (or "unpack," in our idiom) their reality, coming to a new consciousness of themselves and their relations to this reality (nature and society). Problematization becomes a means, further-more, by which the people together alter their relations to this reality and transform their world. . . . But each alteration of relations, each phase of transformation, requires further problematization; the "overcoming" of contradictions . . . [it] is a continual process (not a discrete act that is completed as a "problem" is "solved").[4]

Thus it becomes clear that we must attempt to identify and wrestle with insolvable or divergent problems. It is apparent that many of the problems we face in continuing education are of this type; moreover, there are some inherent difficulties, as Lloyd points out, when we attempt to solve problems in a mechanistic manner.

As you work your way through this book, you will quickly become aware that many of the problems we discuss are divergent problems. There are no single or final answers to them. That is, we will be giving our attention to two kinds of problems: the convergent problem, which is not yet answered but potentially answerable, and the divergent problem. It should be added that there are occasional instances when one cannot be sure whether a problem is convergent or divergent because experience has not as yet provided sufficient data to determine this point.

For the most part, though, one can easily tell which problems are convergent and which are divergent. Because the field of continuing education is concerned with people and their learning, many of the problems it faces are divergent in nature. One of the greatest problems it has faced is its failure to recognize the existence of these divergent problems. Because the field of continuing education has often attempted to emulate the natural sciences in its approaches to solving problems, it has often avoided or even failed to recognize the existence of the divergent problem. Although the natural sciences have a great contribution to make in solving the problems faced by continuing education, they can deal with only some of them. Yet all the problems must be dealt with—especially those that are insolvable.

BARRIERS TO DEALING WITH PROBLEMS

As an educator of adults, you deal with problems every day; it is an important and necessary part of your work. These problems include such matters as

[4]Arthur Selden Lloyd, "Critical Consciousness and Adult Education: An Exploratory Study on Freire's Concept of Conscientization," unpublished M.S. thesis, University of Wisconsin—Madison, 1974. Also see Paulo Freire, *Education for Critical Consciousness*, Seabury, New York, 1973, p. ix.

convincing decision makers of the importance of a program you are working on, handling complaints brought by disgruntled participants in a program, deciding whether a low-enrollment workshop should be dropped, and determining how to respond to a participant who insists on monopolizing your time before, during, and after the sessions you are conducting. You can't avoid dealing with these problems, for they are integral to your work, particularly if you work for an agency or institution that sponsors continuing education programs.

But people in continuing education often avoid dealing with what I refer to as the more basic problems. As I said in the preface to this book, I mean to include under "basic problems" those related to the adult as a learner, the field of continuing education and what it is, the purposes of continuing education, the means and methods of continuing education, the content or curriculum of continuing education, and research approaches.

Why do many people in continuing education avoid dealing with the more basic problems? Let's look at several reasons.

Theory–Practice Conflict

Without question, those working in the field of continuing education are practical people. Every day they deal with practical problems faced by practical people. To suggest to them that they could profit by dealing with more basic problems is to suggest that the practical problems they deal with every day are unimportant. The old argument of theory versus practice rises up once more. By talking about more basic problems, we may appear to be talking about theoretical problems and thus to be trying to push aside the problems of practice.

The problems we will be discussing in this book *are* of a more theoretical nature. But they are nevertheless extremely practical problems as well.

If, for example, you have worked through the problem of what it is that we are trying to accomplish in the field of continuing education, you will probably have less difficulty when you are faced with the everyday question of planning a continuing education program. By working through the more basic problems, we can build a foundation for working with the everyday problems.

Working on fundamental problems can also help us see the relationships among many of the everyday problems we face. Too often, we tend to see these everyday problems in isolation from one another. Dealing with fundamentals can help us tie them together.

Working on basic problems can also help us see the relationship of our work to that of others; ultimately, it can give more meaning to our roles as educators of adults.[5]

Thus the separation of fundamental or theoretical problems from practical

---

[5]For a further discussion of the practical nature of philosophic questions, see Apps, op. cit., pp. 3–6.

problems is a false one. Just as we cannot separate scientific and philosophic questions, we also need to consider theoretical and practical concerns jointly. There can be no integrated practice unless we address theoretical questions. Nor can theoretical problems have any relevance if we fail to address and attend to practical matters. In this perspective, the basic problems with which we will be dealing in this book are highly practical and closely related to the everyday tasks faced by all of us who work in continuing education.

Following this line of reasoning, it doesn't make sense to say that we have insufficient time or money to work on basic problems. Working on basic problems of the type we are discussing will, in the long run, help us save both time and money while also providing the other benefits mentioned above. If we deal with basic problems adequately, we are at the same time dealing with many applied problems to which the basic problems are directly related.

Avoidance of Problems

Many people simply avoid dealing with difficult problems. At least three facts help to explain this type of behavior.

1. Many people avoid working on basic problems because other priorities of work take precedence. This is particularly true if the problem is of a more basic nature—that is, of the type we are discussing in this book.
2. Some people set problems aside deliberately, in the belief that these questions will somehow resolve themselves or that they are the responsibility of others. The latter is an example of the dependency on specialists and experts that we discuss below.
3. Occasionally a person, after looking at a problem briefly, concludes that there is no single answer and that the problem therefore cannot be solved. This person then sets the problem aside as too perplexing and not worth working on. If a problem has no potential for solution, why waste energy on it?

Dependence on Impulse or Whim

Some people avoid dealing with problems because they imagine that they will be able to come up with solutions effortlessly. These people seem to believe that if they do nothing about a problem, the solution *will come to them*.

These people are not to be confused with those who know the power of intuition and the insight that results from it. Intuition and insight—the creative solution to a problem—usually comes only after careful, long, and arduous work. Intuition does not occur without factual input and without in-depth attention. Thus intuition should not be confused with impulse or whim. More will be said about intuition later, when we discuss research approaches in continuing education.

Dependence on Experts and Specialists

Many people in our society fail to work on basic problems because they depend on experts or specialists. We have come to depend on others to help us with our difficulties. When we have a difficult problem or question, we tend immediately to feel that the answer must be "out there" someplace, in the head of some expert or stored in a computer bank. Or, if the answer is not now available, we need only alert the proper expert to the problem and the answer will be forthcoming.

What happens is this. People with problems believe that their task is to search for the experts with the answers rather than try to analyze the questions themselves. This is not to make the naïve claim that there is no place for experts and specialists. We are not suggesting that each person should try to solve problems that others have already solved. What we *are* saying is that a person with a fundamental problem should first analyze and try to deal with the problem alone before going in search for help from experts and specialists.

Too often, we tend to search for answers before we know the questions. With the tremendous development of facts (answers) in our society, we have many answers in search of questions. We must be careful to avoid being seduced by an attractive answer before we have carefully thought about the nature of our problem.

Why do many people in our society depend on experts and specialists for answers? Perhaps our educational system, with its emphasis on transmitting and storing facts, encourages us to search for stored answers rather than to learn how to think for ourselves. Then too, we are part of a high-technology society which promotes the notion that everything has a technical solution which the "experts" can find. Our purpose here, however, is not to explain *why* people depend on specialists and experts but merely to recognize the fact that they do. What are the consequences of this attitude?

1. *People with questions become so intent on searching for answers that they do not take time to reflect on the questions themselves.* They may be searching for the answer to a question that is not the real question at all or, as we explained above, that may be unanswerable. Let's look at a hypothetical situation. As an administrator of a community adult education program, you notice that the attendance level for the classes held by one of your instructors has fallen off rather dramatically this past year. You immediately conclude that the instructor has lost effectiveness and must be replaced. Your question, then, is "How can I effectively replace this instructor?" After a moment's reflection on this situation, you decide that a better question would be, "Why have the student enrollments for this instructor's courses decreased in recent months?"

This is, of course, a simple situation. Yet failure to reflect on a question before searching for solutions is a rather common occurrence.

Another example is the graduate student faced with a term paper assignment and a deadline for finishing it. Let's say the student is interested in writing about participation in adult education programs. Immediately the student goes to the adult education literature and searches for everything available on participation by adults in educational programs. The student writes a paper which has a bibliography that is two pages long, plus a string of footnotes on each page of the manuscript. The student is astounded when the professor does not comment favorably on the paper, particularly in light of all the work that has gone into producing it. What the student has not done at the outset is decide on the question to be answered. What *about* adults participating in adult education programs? What specifically is the question? By going to the experts (at least those who have written on the topic of participation), the student has accomplished little.

2. *The answer to the question often doesn't fit.* In our society, there are many people who implicitly believe in the concept of *interchangeable answers*. That is, they believe that one answer will fit many questions.

An analogy is a widely advertised multipurpose food cutter. It will, it is claimed, slice potatoes, dice carrots, sliver cucumbers, shred cabbage, and cut radishes into the shape of rosebuds. One instrument for many tasks. One answer to many questions. No one considers the possibility that, once the gadget has been purchased, it may shred cabbage quite well but completely mutilate radishes.

For the person with a question, the tendency is to go to the "answer bank" where the experts and specialists have stored their multipurpose answers and pull out the one that seems to fit best. Why waste time working on the question when answers are so readily available?

There are major pitfalls when this approach is followed. On the surface, the person's question is sufficiently similar to the one posed by the expert or specialist that the answer would seem to fit. However, careful analysis of a question often suggests that it is not sufficiently similar to the one worked on by the expert and that therefore the answer doesn't fit.

The notion that there are multipurpose answers is largely a myth. Take the example of the dual-purpose cow, which was once recommended to farmers as the answer to the question of how to produce more milk *and* more meat, both at the same time.

At first glance, this dual-purpose animal seemed to be the ideal answer. If a farmer could raise but one breed of cattle, he could produce more milk for sale. When the animals no longer produced milk, they could be sold for meat. And the bull calves produced by these cattle could be sold for beef too—not for veal, as was commonly done with dairy bull calves.

As might be guessed, the animals never amounted to much. Bred to produce both meat and milk at higher levels than dairy cows or beef cows, the dual-purpose cow, as it turned out, produced neither meat nor milk at acceptable levels.

3. *The broader consequence of dependence on specialists and experts is dependency itself.*

In continuing education, we write and talk about personal freedom and autonomy. We believe that the purpose of education is to give the student a sense of personal freedom. We also maintain that an important goal of continuing education programs is to teach the participants how to deal with their own problems rather than depending on others to provide answers. The seeking of answers from experts and specialists contradicts this basic premise of continuing education for adults. If we believe that one of our purposes in continuing education is to help people become more self-directed, then we must help them learn how to deal with questions in a self-directed way. And we, as educators of adults, must provide an example by not being dependent ourselves.

4. *By being dependent on experts and specialists, people fail to appreciate the proper role of these individuals.*

Experts and specialists are needed in society and in continuing education, although—by now—the reader may have concluded that they are not necessary and that people should answer all their questions by themselves. This, of course, is absurd.

Our argument is that each individual should take responsibility for his or her own questions. People should analyze their questions carefully. They should rely on their own information insofar as they have information to answer their questions, go to colleagues and friends for information to fill in any gaps, and look upon experts and specialists as additional sources of information to feed into the process of reasoning out an answer. Experts, specialists, people with experience in the question area, and public or university libraries are all sources of information that may be helpful in working on a given question. But the person asking the question should control the process of working on it.

SUMMARY

The concept of *problem* presents difficulties for many people. We define a problem as questions raised for inquiry, solution, or both. We examined the concept of *problem* from three perspectives: (1) the relationship of a problem to science and philosophy; (2) the relationship of the problem to the past, the present, or to the future; and (3) the solvability or insolvability of the problem—whether it is a convergent or a divergent problem. We emphasized the need for people in continuing education to identify and work on divergent problems—that is, those which are not solvable. Because continuing education is concerned with people and their growth and learning, the potential benefit to be derived from working on divergent problems is great.

Finally, we explored several barriers that prevent many people in continuing education from working on basic problems they face. We identified the conflict between theory and practice—an old argument but a continuing barrier.

We pointed out that some people often avoid dealing with basic problems because other priorities of their work take precedence. Others respond to problems on impulse or whim, and many depend on experts and specialists for the answers to the basic problems in the field of continuing education. We argue, however, that each individual should take responsibility for clarifying his or her questions before asking for help from others.

SECTION II

THE PARTICIPANTS

Any discussion of continuing education will very soon concern itself with those who participate in this type of education. Many studies of the characteristics of adult learners have been done—their ages, formal education, income levels, motivations for learning, and the like. Answers to these questions are important for those who work in continuing education, particularly that which is institutionally sponsored.

But, even more important, it is essential for those of us who work in continuing education to examine the basic characteristics of human beings. By "basic characteristics," I allude to such opposing viewpoints of human beings (1) as advanced forms of animal life and (2) as essentially different from other animal life. The viewpoint we decide to support will have a profound effect on our performance as educators of adults.

In Chapter 3, these two broad and opposing viewpoints about human beings will be examined. In Chapter 4, the question of what constitutes adulthood will be explored, particularly from the perspective of differences between children and adults.

CHAPTER 3

Points of View About Human Beings

Why do we have problems understanding human beings? Why do we spend time considering this question when other seemingly more important problems beg for attention?

Certainly our understanding of human beings and particularly human adults is crucial to everything we do as educators of adults. As educators, we enter the lives of other people. Sometimes we do this informally, as is done by community educators. At other times, we are much more formal, organizing classes, courses, workshops, and the like. We are, directly or indirectly, affecting the lives of others. What we believe about them as people is crucial to the outcome of what we do. Can we as responsible, concerned educators do our work properly without first examining the most fundamental of our assumptions—that is, those about the nature of the people with whom we work? The answer to this question seems obvious, yet educators of adults often fail to see the importance of reflecting on a responsible answer.

We all have assumptions about human nature. We may never have attempted to write these down; we may never have thought consciously about them. But nevertheless we have them and they influence our actions.

I teach a course designed to assist educators of adults analyze and develop further their working philosophies of continuing education. One unit in the course is concerned with the nature of adults. Most class participants, particularly in the early stages of the course, see the section on adults as least important. They want to move on and analyze continuing education institutions, teaching–learning approaches, and the roles and functions of the educator of adults. In a way, this reaction is understandable. People taking my course, like most educators of adults, are action-oriented. Many of them have recently left a continuing education assignment where they were responsible for organizing or teaching programs for adults. They view a discussion of the nature of adults as *too abstract, too impractical, too limited in available research materials, too far from what the everyday educator of adults needs to be concerned with, and often a question which defies a single, precise answer.*

In this chapter we will examine two broad viewpoints about human beings: (1) that they are essentially related to other life forms and (2) that they are essentially different from other life forms. The first orientation may be either *organismic* or *mechanistic*. The second view—that humans are essentially different from other life forms—is designated the *humanistic* view.

VIEWS OF HUMANITY

What are human beings? This is one of the oldest questions people have asked of themselves and continue to ask. How are we different from other life forms, particularly from other forms of animal life?

These questions have been asked by philosophers, scientists, and artists down through the ages. They might properly be designated as divergent questions (see previous chapter), for there are no easy, single answers.

As we examine the literature on various views of humanity, we discover two prominent positions. The first can be illustrated by a continuum with human beings at one end and the lower life forms at the other.

| Lower life forms | Plants | Animals | Humans |

Figure 1   The continuum of life

The logic of this position is that human beings, although they represent the most advanced form of life, are in essence no different from other life forms.

Those who support the second position argue that human beings have inherent qualities and traits that prevent us from putting them on a continuum with other life. These people quickly admit that we do share certain traits with other life forms. But we have other traits that are clearly human and not shared with any other life form, no matter how advanced. These traits which are not shared with other life forms are those that profoundly characterize human beings, it is argued.

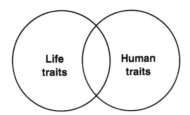

Figure 2   Life traits and human traits

The circle on the left represents life traits, while the circle on the right represents human traits. The area where the two circles overlap represents those characteristics that humans and other life forms, particularly animals, have in common. Let us look at these two positions—the *continuum-of-life* position and the *humanistic* position—in greater detail.

Human Beings on a Continuum with All Life

Several writers openly describe human beings as higher forms of animal life but in essence no different from other animals. Some of the descriptions are purely biological, others are psychological. For instance, Sir George Pickering, a professor of medicine at Oxford University, writes about the human being as "the most successful animal in our universe as judged by the usual criteria such as total weight or volume."[1]

Pickering gives three reasons why this is so: (1) our upper limbs are unspecialized and the thumb is mobile, so we can grasp objects in our hands; (2) we have binocular vision, which allows us to focus our gaze on a specific object and follow it in three-dimensional space when it moves; and (3) we have large brains and can "learn from experiences more quickly and in much more complicated detail than any other animals."[2]

Pickering summarizes the implications of these three characteristics: Human beings have

> . . . *learned to make tools, and later, machines, which enormously improve the range and precision with which [they] can control [their] environment. But perhaps [their] most valuable asset has been speech and its written equivalent, writing. Most higher animals communicate with one another. Man is unique in the complexity and precision of the information he conveys to his fellows. . . . Because man's brain has a*

[1]Sir George Pickering in F. W. Jessup (ed.), *Lifelong Learning: A Symposium on Continuing Education*, Pergamon, London, 1969, p. 2.

[2]Ibid., p. 2.

large capacity for storage, and because of speech and writing skills, knowledge and ideas are transmitted to succeeding generations who perfect them.[3]

Pickering comes at the question of human nature from a purely biological perspective. Others, particularly the psychologists, have looked at the question from a different angle. For example, William R. Looft says,

Everyone carries around within him a model of man—a personalized conception of the nature of human nature, a common-sense notion about 'the way people are.' He may not be able to verbalize precisely just what his personal theory about human nature is, but he clearly has one, for it is implicit in what he does for, and about other people.[4]

Looft goes on to say that psychologists, being no different from anyone else, "accept, implicitly or explicity, a model of human nature; it is used as a guide and a rationale for both their theoretical and empirical work."[5]

As a result of accepting different assumptions about the nature of humanity, psychologists have developed psychological models of human development that appear quite different from one another.

As it turns out, once we examine several psychological models of human development, the fundamental issue seems to be one of external versus internal influence. That is, does developmental change occur in human beings as a result of changes inside the organism or because of changes external to it?

Looft describes two basic orientations: *organismic* models, which refer to changes within people because of changes within the organism, and *mechanistic* models, which refer to changes within people in response to changes in their environment.[6]

Frank Goble links the internal orientation to the work of Sigmund Freud and the external orientation to John B. Watson's and B. F. Skinner's work. Though these two orientations are in many ways extremely different from one another, they do have in common one important characteristic. Both the organismic and the mechanistic perspectives describe the human being as another type of

[3]Ibid., p. 3.

[4]William R. Looft, "Socialization and Personality Throughout the Life Span: An Examination of Contemporary Psychological Approaches," in Paul B. Baltes and K. Warner Schaie (eds.), *Life-Span Developmental Psychology: Personality and Socialization*, Academic, New York, 1973, p. 26.

[5]Ibid., p. 26.

[6]Ibid., pp. 29–30.

animal, "with no essential differences from [other] animals. . . ."[7] Let's look briefly at each perspective.

The Freudian View Sigmund Freud (1856–1939) advanced one of the most influential theories of human behavior in recent history. Freud was greatly influenced by Charles Darwin and believed that human beings were the product of accidental evolution. He made it clear in his work that human beings were animals and no more than animals. But

> In the course of his development toward culture man acquired a dominating position over his fellow creatures in the animal kingdom. Not content with this supremacy, however, he began to place a gulf between his nature and theirs. He denied the possession of reason to them, and to himself he attributed an immortal soul, and made claims to a divine descent which permitted him to annihilate the bond of community between him and the animal kingdom. . . . we all know that, little more than a half century ago, the researches of Charles Darwin, his collaborators and predecessors put an end to this presumption on the part of man. Man is not a being different from animals or superior to them; he himself originates in the animal race and is related more closely to some of its members and more distantly to others.[8]

According to Freud, our basic, genetic, instinctual drives come from our animal origins. Freud was interested in the unconscious mind and particularly its influence on human behavior.

Freud talked about the "id," which was his word for the unconscious animal instincts. These unconscious instincts (the id) are, according to Freud, powerful, antisocial, and irrational.

Freud also talked about the "superego," which was in constant conflict with the id. The superego's function is to repress the natural raw instincts. The human being is not born with a superego, which is, rather, acquired, usually as the parent teaches the child the customs and morals of society.

Freud argued that the basic direction of a person's life is determined in early childhood, usually by about age five. Occasionally, according to Freud, this basic direction can be altered by a method of therapy which he called psychoanalysis.

[7]Frank G. Goble, *The Third Force*, Grossman, New York, 1970, p. 8.

[8]Sigmund Freud, *On Creativity and the Unconscious*, Harper & Row, New York, 1958, pp. 5–6.

Freud's view of human beings was quite negative. He wrote,

> . . . *men are not gentle creatures who want to be loved, and who at the most can defend themselves if they are attacked; they are, on the contrary, creatures among whose instinctual endowment is to be reckoned a powerful share of aggressiveness. As a result, their neighbor is for them not only a potential helper or sexual object, but also someone who tempts them to satisfy their aggressiveness on him, to exploit his capacity for work without compensation, to use him sexually without his consent, to seize his possessions, to humiliate him, to cause him pain, to torture and to kill him.*[9]

Freud held that people *could* demonstrate moral or unselfish behavior, but only at the expense of suppressing the id. In other words, Freud saw morality and altruism as unnatural.

As we study Freud, we conclude that he considered the human being at birth to be a bundle of instinctual drives. The struggle of the ego to bring the drives of the id, the needs of the superego, and the experience of reality into balance determines the individual's later behavior. Cultural and societal influences, to a lesser or greater extent, cause people to suppress their natural instinctual drives and display behavior that could be described as good or moral. This suppression of instinctual drives is learned; it does not occur naturally.

The Behavioristic View   The general theory of behaviorism was developed by John B. Watson (1878–1958). Watson's mission was to make the study of humans as scientific and as objective as possible. Today, the foremost proponent of behaviorism is B. F. Skinner of Harvard University. What is the behavioristic view of humans?

Floyd W. Matson summarizes the basic assumptions of behaviorism as follows:

> . . . *the assumption as to human nature is that it is malleable clay awaiting the hand of the behavioral artisan, and the ambition as to the future is to design a technology that will—not enhance the freedom and dignity of individuals—but shape the behavior of members of a group so that they will function smoothly for the benefit of all.*[10]

[9]Sigmund Freud, *Civilization and Its Discontents*, Norton, New York, 1961, p. 58.
[10]Floyd W. Matson, *The Idea of Man*, Dell, New York, 1976, pp. 125–126.

As mentioned above, the behaviorists adhere to a strictly "scientific" approach in their study of human beings. They have dropped from their vocabulary such terms as "perception," "image," "desire," "purpose," "freedom," and "dignity," which they consider as subjective and incapable of precise definition. By adhering to a narrowly defined scientific approach, the behaviorists accept a deterministic view of human nature.

Skinner writes, "If we are to use the methods of science in the field of human affairs we must assume that behavior is lawful and determined . . . that what a man does is the result of specifiable conditions and that once these conditions have been discovered, we can anticipate and to some extent determine his actions."[11]

The intent of the scientific efforts of the behaviorists is to discover conditions that predict human behavior. Given certain conditions, we can anticipate, within an agreed upon range of probability, what human behaviors will result.

Gordon W. Allport traces the behaviorists' roots back to the philosophy of John Locke. Locke assumed that the individual's mind was a tabula rasa (or blank slate) at birth; content and structure were acquired only through the impact of external influences. Allport summarizes several assumptions of the Lockean position:

> . . . what is external and visible is more fundamental than what is not. . . . Learning is regarded as the substitution of one effective stimulus for another or of one response for another. . . . What is small and molecular . . . is more fundamental than what is large and molar. . . . What is earlier is more fundamental than what is late in development.[12]

The basic difference between the Freudian and behavioristic views centers upon their respective hypotheses regarding the source of the influences that shape human behavior. Freud emphasizes the deep inner drives and urges— the animal instincts—as influencers of behavior, while the behaviorists emphasize the external, environmental influences. But in both cases the human being is viewed as an advanced animal that is not free.

Skinner writes,

> The hypothesis that man is not free is essential to the application of

[11]B. F. Skinner, *Science and Human Behavior*, Macmillan, New York, 1953, p. 6.
[12]Gordon W. Allport, *Becoming*, Yale University Press, New Haven, Conn., 1955, pp. 7–10.

scientific method to the study of human behavior. The free inner man who is held responsible for the behavior of the external biological organism is only a prescientific substitute for the kinds of causes which are discovered in the course of a scientific analysis. All these alternative causes lie outside the individual. . . . These are the things which make the individual behave as he does. For them he is not responsible, and for them it is useless to praise or blame him.[13]

In addition to their agreement that human beings are only advanced forms of animal life, both Freudians and behaviorists agree that the early years of a person's life have considerable influence on his or her adult years.

Insofar as the behaviorists view human beings as advanced animals, Skinner writes: "The only differences I expect to see revealed between the behavior of rats and man (aside from enormous differences in complexity) lie in the field of verbal behavior."[14]

Another way of thinking about human beings as externally controlled is to think of them as machines.[15] With the coming of the technological revolution, the physical work load of many people has been lightened. But while their physical drudgery has decreased, these same people now tend to take on the characteristics of their machines. The machine, designed to aid its master, has become master. The shift in control has been rapid and subtle. Who has not heard, "We can't do this because the computer won't accept the information," or "We can't come to your meeting—there's a football game on TV that night." We all know of thousands of such examples.

As a result of this quiet revolution, this shift between master and servant, people feel powerless, lonely, anxious, passive, and dependent. When the electrical power goes out, society stops functioning.

People feel like tiny feathers in a windstorm, blowing this way and that, never stopping but never going anywhere either.

There is tragedy as well as irony in the observation that, at the same time as man collectively is gaining control over his physical world and his evolutionary fate, man individually feels himself to be losing control over his personal world and his private life. Both phenomena, moreover, are

---

[13]Skinner, op. cit., pp. 447–448.

[14]Quoted in Floyd W. Matson, *The Broken Image: Man, Science, and Society*, Braziller, New York, 1964.

[15]See Lewis Mumford, *The Myth of the Machine: The Pentagon of Power*, Harcourt Brace Jovanovich, New York, 1964, 1970, for an eloquent discussion of this idea.

traceable to the same source: both are products of the technological ethos.[16]

In summary, as we look back on the continuum of life, those who argue that human beings are no more than advanced animals tend to take two somewhat opposing positions. Some believe that we consist of a bundle of instinctual drives that determine our behavior; this is the so called *internal* (organismic) orientation. Then, there are others who believe that we are totally influenced by our environment; this is the *external* (mechanistic) orientation. The Freudian approach represents the internal orientation, while the external orientation is represented by behaviorism.

Within the latter group are those who, although they may not explicitly say so, see people as machines and tend to look upon them just as they would on any other machine.

Let us now turn to the second broad view of human nature—that which suggests that we are animals but, at the same time, also different from animals.

2053813

The Humanistic View

So far we have pointed out the two basic perspectives on human beings, the organismic or internal orientation and the mechanistic or external orientation. A logical conclusion at this point would be to combine both orientations for a rounded picture.

But as we will argue here, both these positions, even when combined, tell us only about those characteristics that humanity shares with animal life. The humanistic view goes further and argues that there are dimensions of human life that are profoundly different from those of animal life. In fact, as the argument goes, it is precisely those characteristics that we do *not* share with animals that make us human.

E. F. Schumacher is one of those who argues for the existence of unique human characteristics. He describes four levels of existence: (1) inanimate matter—the mineral level, (2) the plant level, (3) the animal level, and (4) the human level.

According to Schumacher, each level has some of the characteristics of the level that precedes it but also others, in addition, that clearly separate it from the preceding levels. For example, Schumacher says that level 2, that of plants, includes many characteristics of the mineral level *plus* life. Level 3, the animal level, includes the characteristics of minerals and plants and, in addition,

---

[16]Matson, *The Idea of Man*, p. 75.

consciousness. And level 4, the human level, includes all the preceding *plus* self-awareness.

Following Schumacher's line of reasoning, human beings have the qualities of minerals as well as life, consciousness, and self-awareness. The key to understanding Schumacher's argument is in his distinction between *consciousness* and *self-awareness*. Schumacher says, "What has to be fully understood is that there are differences in kind, and not simply in degree, between the *powers* of life, consciousness and self-awareness."[17]

Schumacher defines consciousness in this way: "It is easy to recognize consciousness in a dog, a cat, or a horse, if only because they can be knocked unconscious: the processes of life continue as in a plant, although the animal has lost its peculiar powers."[18]

As for self-awareness, Schumacher says,

> *This power z [self-awareness] has undoubtedly a great deal to do with the fact that man is not only able to think but is also able to be aware of his thinking. Consciousness and intelligence, as it were, recoil upon themselves. There is not merely a conscious being, but a being capable of being conscious of its consciousness; not merely a thinker, but a thinker capable of watching and studying his own thinking. There is something able to say "I" and to direct consciousness in accordance with its own purposes, a master or controller, a power at a higher level than consciousness itself. This power z [self-awareness], consciousness recoiling upon itself, opens up unlimited possibilities of purposeful learning, investigating, exploring, and of formulating and accumulating knowledge.[19]*

For Schumacher, the characteristic that clearly sets humanity apart from the three other levels of being that he describes is self-awareness. He also wants us to understand that self-awareness is not something lying on a continuum with consciousness; it is of an entirely different nature.

Other terms that are often used to describe our humanistic characteristics include "active nature;" "individuality;" "freedom;" "dynamic internal world;" "search for meaning;" "time, symbols, and emotions," and "the social dimension."

Active Nature In the previous section, we said that Locke saw human nature as essentially passive. Another famous philosopher, G. W. Leibnitz, saw human

[17]E. F. Schumacher, *A Guide for the Perplexed*, Harper & Row, New York, 1977, p. 21.
[18]Ibid., p. 16.
[19]Ibid., p. 17.

nature as active. Many contemporary humanistic writers trace their arguments back to Leibnitz. Allport, for example, claims that:

> *To Leibnitz the intellect was perpetually active in its own right, addicted to rational problem solving, and bent on manipulating sensory data according to its own inherent nature. For Locke the organism was reactive when stimulated; for Leibnitz it was self-propelled. . . .*
>
> *The Leibnitzian tradition . . . maintains that the person is not a collection of acts, nor simply the locus of acts; the person is the source of acts. And activity itself is not conceived as agitation resulting from pushes by internal or external stimulation. It is purposive. To understand what a person is . . . is always to refer to what he may be in the future, for every state of the person is pointed in the direction of future possibilities.*[20]

Individuality   Allport emphasizes the individual nature of each person, which results from his or her human characteristics. Where in animals and plants there is some individuality, in humans the individuality is enormous.

> *Unlike plants and lower animals, man is not merely a creature of cell structure, tropism, and instinct; he does not live his life by repeating, with trivial variation, the pattern of his species. Nature's heavy investment in individuality stands forth chiefly in* homo sapiens. *While we may recognize individual differences among dogs or varying strains of temperament among rats, still their lives in all essential particulars are regulated by their membership in a species. Man alone has the capacity to vary his biological needs extensively and to add to them countless psychogenic needs reflecting in part his culture (no other creature has a culture), and in part his own style of life (no other creature worries about his life-style).*[21]

Freedom   Matson emphasizes freedom as the essential characteristic that separates us from other life forms. The human being is "a free agent, a creative actor on the world stage—which is not only distinct from the bestial and mechanical modes but profoundly opposed to both. The central point . . . is that man is free, in a sense and to a degree unknown to animal, vegetable, or mineral."[22]

[20]Allport, op. cit., pp. 8, 12.

[21]Allport, op. cit., p. 22.

[22]Matson, *The Idea of Man*, p. xx.

Matson compares the humanistic view with the views held by the Freudians and the behaviorists. "In place of the behaviorist axiom that the causes of man's conduct are to be found in his environment, and of the Freudian axiom that those causes are to be found in his unconscious, the new psychology of humanism proposes the outrageous hypothesis that man may have a directive hand in his own life, that he may know something about what he is doing and seeking. . . ."[23]

Michael Littleford also emphasized freedom in describing an essential characteristic that sets human beings apart from other animal life, but he uses the word "choice."

Because he is aware of himself and the world, man, at least subjectively experiences the reality and necessity of choice. . . . It is true that from the point of view of the acting scientist the individual appears to have no choice. However, according to the Humanists, this is a paradox with which we must live. Choice is a core experience in a person's internal life. . . . [24]

Uncertainty and risk accompany choice. The future is always uncertain and we are never completely sure that the right choice has been made. As a result of this dilemma, we experience guilt, anguish, despair, and anxiety. A characteristic of the human condition is the constant tension between the joy of choosing how one will reach toward potentialities and the despair and tragedy that accompany the uncertainty and risk of choice.

To live docilely and avoid choosing—that is, to let others make choices for us—seems to be a reasonable approach toward avoiding the uncertainties and the risks that accompany choosing for oneself and the ultimate tragedy of making a wrong choice. But not choosing is not accepting the uniqueness that makes one human. Thus, according to this position, people who accept a life where others make choices for them live at a level that is less than the fully human.

Dynamic Internal World Another human characteristic relates to those elusive and mysterious inner workings of the human mind that Lewis Mumford calls the "dynamic internal world." (This is not to be confused with the organismic view described earlier.) Mumford writes,

[23]Ibid., p. 207.

[24]Michael Littleford, "Some Philosophical Assumptions of Humanistic Psychology," *Educational Theory*, vol. 20, no. 3, pp. 234–235, Summer 1970.

The existence in man of a dynamic internal world, whose essential nature cannot be probed by any instrument, and can be known only when it finds expression in gestures and symbols and constructive activities, is a mystery as profound as the focus that binds together the components of the atom and accounts for the character and behavior of the elements. . . . In man that mystery can be experienced, but not described, still less explained: for the mind cannot mirror itself from within. Only by getting outside itself does it become conscious of its inwardness.[25]

Search for Meaning   Victor E. Frankl and James R. Royce emphasize the "search for meaning" as one of the important characteristics that separate us from other life forms. Royce believes that the search for meaning in life is a constant quest, beginning when a child first becomes aware of life's mystery and continuing until the adult faces the mystery of death.[26]

Frankl, as a result of his long-standing concern about the importance of searching for meaning in life, developed a form of therapy he calls "logotherapy." He compares this with Freud's psychoanalysis as follows:

Logotherapy deviates from psychoanalysis insofar as it considers man as a being whose main concern consists in fulfilling a meaning and in actualizing values, rather than in mere gratification and satisfaction of drives and instincts, the mere reconciliation of the conflicting claims of the id, ego, and superego, or mere adaptation and adjustment to the society and environment.[27]

Time, Symbols, and Emotions   Human beings have the capacity to tell time and to recognize that there is a past as well as a future. They have the capacity to use symbols such as words and numbers, and they can think abstractly using such symbolic terms as "beauty," "reason," and "goodness." Human beings also have the capacity to express love and hate and to feel guilt and shame, elation and joy, tenderness and compassion.

Carl Rogers poetically summarizes the uniqueness of humans this way: A person is "a stream of becoming, not a finished product . . . a fluid process, not

[25]Mumford, op. cit., p. 418.
[26]Joseph R. Royce, *The Encapsulated Man*, Van Nostrand, Princeton, N.J., 1964, p. 1.
[27]Victor E. Frankl, *Man's Search for Meaning*, Beacon, New York, 1963, p. 164.

a fixed and static entity; a flowing river of change, not a block of solid material; a continually changing constellation of potentialities, not a fixed quantity of traits."[28]

The Social Dimension Human beings are integrally related to others of their kind. As Freire points out,

To be human is to engage in relationships with others and with the world. It is to experience that world as an objective reality, independent of oneself, capable of being known. Animals, submerged within reality, cannot relate to it; they are creatures of mere contacts. *But man's separateness from and openness to the world distinguishes him as a being of* relationships. *Men, unlike animals, are not only* in *the world but with the world.*[29]

Human beings are not only *influenced by* but have the potential for *influencing* their social settings. Unfortunately, because they are so malleable, they are easily seduced into accepting a particular form of human relationships in society without questioning the form. As Erich Fromm points out, "man defines his humanity in terms of the society with which he identifies himself."[30]

But the situation that Fromm points out does not negate our capacity to change our society or our world. This is a profound capacity that is uniquely human.

THE PROBLEM FOR CONTINUING EDUCATION

So far we have presented three viewpoints on human beings: the organismic, mechanistic, and humanistic perspectives. Educators of adults (all educators, for that matter) tend to subscribe to or lean toward one position more than the others. If we reflect back on the discussion of divergent and convergent problems, it would appear that the question of how human beings are viewed is a divergent question with at least three answers. Each of the three answers has strong advocates who argue that their answer is the correct one.

It also becomes apparent, as we analyze the literature of the three viewpoints, that the mechanistic view represented by the behaviorists and the organismic view represented by the psychoanalysts have been given the

[28]Carl R. Rogers, *On Becoming a Person*, Houghton Mifflin, Boston, 1961, p. 122.
[29]Paulo Freire, *Education for Critical Consciousness*, Seabury, New York, 1973, p. 3.
[30]Erich Fromm, *The Revolution of Hope*, Harper & Row, New York, 1968, p. 56.

greater prominence. Only in recent years have educators begun to discuss a *third force*, or a humanistic view.

Reasons for Prominence of Behavioristic and Psychoanalytic Viewpoints

As we have pointed out above, both the behavioristic and the psychoanalytic viewpoints assume that human beings are essentially only higher forms of animal life and no more. By accepting this assumption about human life, it is possible to follow the research approaches of natural science in studying human beings. As we point out in the two final chapters of this book, where we discuss research in continuing education, many researchers prefer, for a number of reasons, to follow the natural science format. By assuming that human beings are higher-level animals, they can consistently follow this approach.

A practical reason why many educators of adults have followed a behavioristic approach to continuing education involves what might be called the "bandwagon syndrome." When a new idea in education comes along, educators are quick to adopt it, often without giving much thought to the assumptions behind it. For example, over the past several years educators at every level have considered such fads as *computerized instruction*, *programmed learning*, *back to the basics*, *learning by objectives*, *and competency-based education*.

As the fads are developed and promoted, many educators are quick to try out the new ideas. After all, who wants to be viewed as one who avoids innovation? The result is that many educators adopt new approaches to the planning and execution of educational programs without ever thinking about the underlying assumptions.

It is easy to understand why the overworked educator will latch onto a new idea without careful examination. Since many adult education agencies and institutions—as well as the publishers of educational materials—have openly advocated the new ideas, educators have had little choice but to use them.

Often too, harried educators will accept a new idea at face value simply because they have no time to explore the underlying assumptions. Thus these educators really don't know what the implications of the new idea might be. They may agree that human beings are unique, having characteristics that are clearly different from those of animals. But such an educator will organize a learning activity that is clearly behavioristic in every way—for example, a tightly organized competency-based program. The obvious contradiction between belief and action is not evident to the educator. Once one takes the time to reflect on beliefs and actions, these contradictions become obvious. But in the rush to put on programs, such time for reflection is clearly a luxury.

Narrow Humanistic Viewpoint

Just as there are educators who subscribe to the behavioristic and psychoanalytic viewpoints, there are those who subscribe to a narrow humanistic approach. These people minimize the significance of those traits that human beings share with other forms of life. They want to consider only the features that are unique to humanity and ignore, for example, biological questions. This position is understandable, particularly in view of the relatively small number of people who even concern themselves with the question of which qualities are uniquely human.

Another argument made by those who advocate a narrow humanistic approach is that people are not part of the natural world. This belief, which finds expression in both religious and secular literature, goes on to argue that humanity has the potential to control the world of nature and, in fact, has a divine mandate to do so.

Still another problem with the narrow humanistic approach is its emphasis on individualism and choice. If individualism and choice are viewed narrowly, we see society as merely a collection of individuals pursuing their own personal goals, without concern for the totality.

A Broadened Humanistic Approach

Is it possible to consider all three viewpoints—the behavioristic (mechanistic), psychoanalytic (organismic), and humanistic viewpoints—at the same time? That is, is it possible to transcend the problem, as Schumacher suggests, and as we explained in the previous chapter, so as to accommodate all three viewpoints? We believe that it is not only possible but essential to do so.

In other words, the human being is, at the same time, in part determined (the organismic position), in part influenced by environment (the mechanistic position), and in part purposive and self-directed (the humanistic approach). Each individual does have animal characteristics and these do influence behavior. Sexuality, family life, aggression, aging, and death—these and other characteristics which we share with animals are givens and deserve the attention of those who are concerned about humanity.

The human being is an integral part of the natural world. Though there are many who argue to the contrary, as mentioned above, the advent of the energy crisis and environmental concerns have forced many people to rethink their positions on this issue. More people are coming to realize that we are both apart from the natural world and an integral part of it. Rather than controlling nature, the need is to discover ways of living in harmony with it.

Human beings are also integral parts of their society and their culture and are constantly influenced by societal and cultural forces. They cannot be viewed as standing apart. But, on the other hand, people also have the potential for influencing both their society and their culture.

In addition to being influenced by their animalness and by their environment, human beings also have characteristics that clearly make them unique—that clearly make them human. That is, they are at the same time determined, influenced by their environments, and also free to choose the direction of their lives.

SUMMARY

In this chapter we have focused our attention on points of view about human beings. We presented two alternative positions about them—seeing them (1) on a continuum with all life and (2) in terms of those qualities that set them apart from other living things. For the first position we discussed two variants: the Freudian (organismic) view and the behavioristic (mechanistic) view of human nature. Both the Freudian and the behavioristic views assume human beings to be higher-level animals and no more, although they differ on the source of the primary causes of human behavior.

The humanistic view, while conceding that people have much in common with animals, argues that human beings have qualities that clearly set them apart. These have been described under the headings "active nature;" "individuality;" "freedom;" "dynamic internal world;" "search for meaning;" "time, symbols, and emotions;" and "the social dimension."

Within continuing education, emphasis is often placed on one of the three positions: organismic, mechanistic, or a narrow interpretation of the humanistic viewpoint. We argued that it was an error to adhere to any one of these positions, yet many educators of adults do just that. Particularly, there are a growing number of educators who rely on the behavioristic viewpoint.

It was argued that it is possible to consider all three viewpoints at the same time. Humans are both advanced animals and more than animals. They are influenced by the "animal instincts" (organismic view) and they are also influenced by the environment (mechanistic view). But, in addition to these two influences, they are also self-directed and purposive in their behavior.

SUGGESTED READINGS

Brill, A. A. (ed.): *The Basic Writings of Sigmund Freud*, Modern Library, New York, 1938.

Maslow, Abraham H.: *Toward a Psychology of Being*, Van Nostrand Reinhold, New York, 1968.

Montagu, Ashley: *Man in Process*, New American Library, New York, 1961.

Rose, Anthony L., and Andre Auw: *Growing Up Human*, Harper & Row, New York, 1974.

Skinner, B. F.: *Beyond Freedom and Dignity*, Knopf, New York, 1971.

————: *Walden Two*, Macmillan, New York, 1948.

CHAPTER 4

Characteristics of Adults

In discussing the education of adults with people who are preparing for such teaching positions, we inevitably hear, "But what is an adult? And how is an adult different from a child?" Anyone working in the field of continuing education should have little difficulty in answering those questions—one would think. But the answers become more difficult as education becomes more complex.

Some people have little trouble defining "adult." They simply answer, "An adult is anyone who is older than 18; that's the legal definition, you know." And they are technically correct. But what makes a person of 18 more an adult than one who is, say, 17 years 11 months of age, particularly from the perspective of education?

Some people have tried to answer the question in terms of relationship to family. That is, anyone who is no longer dependent on his or her family for support is an adult. Does this mean that the person who is 23 years old, enrolled in college, and dependent on her family for bed and board is not an adult?

Some who try to define "adult" assume that all adults are essentially the same. An adult is an adult is an adult—just as a rose is a rose is a rose. Though some may be red and some yellow, some wild and some cultivated, all roses are roses.

These are but samples of the many problems in this area. Though we obviously cannot answer the question of "adultness" once and for all, we will attempt to look at various dimensions of the problem. By so doing we would like, or hope, to challenge the reader to move beyond such simple answers as those illustrated above. Rather than attempt to develop a set definition, we will explore various ways of describing adults. We will discuss the idea of life-span development. We will look at several dimensions of life changes. And we will explore the concepts of intelligence and maturity, particularly as they relate to adults.

Let's begin by looking at the problem as a continuation of one we discussed in Chapter 3. We said that human beings have something in common with physical, plant, and animal forms as well as something unique that sets them apart from all the rest of nature.

This uniqueness—the ability to be aware of self, for example—is shared by all people, no matter where they live, no matter what their occupation, no matter what their sex.

But as we look at people—say we observe a group coming out of a movie house on a Saturday evening—we see some who are young, some who are middle aged, and some who are elderly. We observe a great diversity in physical stature and appearance. We conclude that no two individuals in this group are alike. Yet although no two people are the same, they share much in common. Some of these commonalities have to do with age. For example, people who are retired share a great many experiences and interests that are similar. So while each person has qualities that are unique, each also shares common concerns with others.

With this as background, let's begin to explore the question of what actually constitutes adulthood.

AGES AND STAGES

In recent years, a great deal of research has been done on life-span development. The intent of this research is to attempt to predict the kinds of problems that people will face as they go through life. All this research attempts to relate certain events and situations to certain ages (or stages of life). Some of the life-span work tends to focus on biological characteristics, some on psychological characteristics, some on sociological and some on psychosocial characteristics.

In *As You Like It*, Shakespeare wrote about the seven stages of a human life:

the infant mewling and puking . . .
the whining schoolboy . . .
the lover, sighing like a furnace . . .

a soldier, full of strange oaths . . .
the justice, in fair round belly . . .
the sixth age shifts . . . with spectacles on nose . . .
voice turning again toward childish treble . . .
Last scene of all . . .
second childishness . . . Sans teeth, sans eye, sans taste, sans
everything. . . .

Erik Erikson suggests eight stages of what he calls ego development. Erikson sets up his stages in terms of a dichotomy of what happens if a person is successful or unsuccessful in working through, in sequence, the tensions characteristic of the stage in which he or she lives.

Whereas Erikson is age-specific with regard to the developmental areas relating to childhood, he is less specific about adults. He uses three broad groupings: early adulthood, middle adulthood, and late adulthood.

During *early adulthood*, the person, according to Erikson, is faced with the tension between intimacy and isolation. Intimacy means a commitment of self to others, and isolation means avoidance of intimacy. During *middle adulthood*, the person is faced with the tension between generativity and stagnation. Generativity means, in part, being productive and creative for self and others. Stagnation means being nonproductive, excessively self-loving, egocentric. During *late adulthood* the person is faced with resolving the tension between integrity and despair. Integrity includes an appreciation of one's continuity with the past, present, and future—that is, a sense of being complete. Despair indicates that no meaning in life has been found; therefore there is loss of faith in self and others.[1]

Havighurst writes about the developmental tasks faced by people in six different life stages—that is, those of (1) infancy and early childhood, (2) middle childhood, (3) adolescence, (4) early adulthood, (5) middle age, and (6) later maturity.

Examples of developmental tasks for the adult stages are as follows: *Early adulthood*—Selecting a mate, getting started in an occupation: *Middle age*—Achieving adult civic and social responsibility, adjusting to aging parents; *Later maturity*—adjusting to decreasing physical strength and health, adjusting to death of spouse.[2]

Havighurst argues that these developmental tasks must be mastered at each stage of life. Failure to do so will lead to problems in the ensuing stage.

[1]Erik H. Erikson, *Childhood and Society*, 2d ed., Norton, New York, 1963, pp. 247–274.

[2]Robert J. Havighurst, *Developmental Tasks and Education*, 3d ed., McKay, New York, 1972.

Gail Sheehy, drawing on the work of many of the life-span researchers such as Erikson, Gould, and Neugarten, wrote an exceedingly popular book describing what she calls "passages." Her focus, unlike most in the literature, is entirely on adults. She describes six passages in outlining what happens during the adult life span.

1. *Pulling up Roots:* This passage, Sheehy explains, occurs when a person at, about the age of 18, begins to leave home in search of an anticipated occupation. There is increasing separation between self and parents.
2. *The Trying Twenties:* The focus here is on putting aspirations to work, getting started in an occupation, developing the capacity for intimacy, searching out a mentor.
3. *Catch-30:* People approaching age 30 often feel a need to evaluate their lives and take a new look at where they are going. This may mean abandoning a marriage or an occupation.
4. *Rooting and Extending:* In the early thirties, life becomes more settled, more rational. Emphasis is on career ladders and "making it."
5. *The Deadline Decade:* This usually occurs during the middle thirties and continues to about age 45. It is a crossroads time for most people, when the examination of life again becomes crucial. It is the time when people realize that they have lived more than half their lives.
6. *Renewal or Resignation:* Sometime during the mid-forties, some sense of stability is again achieved. For some people, this is an exciting time, for they have discovered new dimensions in their personal lives and their occupations. Others become resigned to less than satisfying marriages and jobs that are going nowhere. "If we have confronted ourselves in the middle passage and found a renewal of purpose around which we are eager to build a more authentic life structure, these may well be the best years."[3]

Although much is being published on life-span development studies, the work is not without its critics. Some of the criticism comes from those who say the life-span work, particularly that which focuses on predetermined personality changes throughout the life span, is too narrow.

Looft writes,

In a world torn between potentials for tremendous humanitarian improvement and massive destruction of humanity, between incredible affluence and rising unemployment, and between communications media that integrate people together and at the same time create

---

[3]Gail Sheehy, *Passages*, Dutton, New York, 1976, pp. 25–32.

cynicism and despair, Freud's sexuality and Erikson's personal identity concerns diminish in importance.[4]

Looft believes that any model for understanding the development of human beings throughout the life-span must take into account the cultural, social, mental, biological, and historical development of humans. "No longer should developmental psychologists focus so exclusively on ontogenetic age functions; each new generation will manifest age trends that are different from those that preceded it, and thus previous empirical endeavors are reduced to exercises in futility."[5]

Looft also admits that one of the primary reasons why the more encompassing approach he suggests may never be adopted is the complexity of the research methodology that is involved.

Neugarten and Datan are also critical of the narrowness of many of the life-span models, noting that "studies of development are more often characterized by a search for a universal sequence of personality change comparable to, if not paced by, the maturational timetable, rather than a search for the sequences of personality changes that can be shown to reflect historical and social events."[6]

Agreeing with Looft, these writers point out that "we lack a set of conceptual tools by which to integrate maturational, psychological, sociological, and historical perspectives on the life cycle."[7]

Time would be one way of integrating life-span work, according to these researchers. They suggest an integration of three kinds of time: (1) life time—the individual's chronological age, (2) social time—the system of age grading and age expectations that shapes the life-cycle, and (3) historical time—"the succession of political, economic, and social events that shape the setting into which the individual is born and make up the dynamic, constantly changing background against which his life is lived."[8]

The approaches suggested by Looft and by Neugarten and Datan are obviously much more complicated for the researcher to contend with. Not only

[4]William R. Looft, "Socialization and Personality Throughout the Life Span: An Examination of Contemporary Psychological Approaches," in Paul B. Baltes and K. Warner Schaie (eds.), *Life-Span Developmental Psychology: Personality and Socialization*, Academic, New York, 1973, p. 50.

[5]Ibid., p. 51.

[6]Bernice L. Neugarten and Nancy Datan, "Sociological Perspectives on the Life Cycle," in Paul B. Baltes and K. Warner Schaie (eds.), *Life-Span Developmental Psychology: Personality and Socialization*, Academic, New York, 1973, p. 54.

[7]Ibid., p. 54.

[8]Ibid., p. 54.

is there a problem with inadequate tools and concepts for carrying out the research but the element of predictability is, by definition, destroyed if we must take into account all the forces that influence an individual at a given time of life. These forces are obviously different during different historical periods. The forces affecting people who were in their twenties during 1941–1945 (World War II) are obviously different from the forces affecting those who are in their twenties today.

But there is still another problem with depending too much on the life-span development work for an understanding of human nature—especially the differences between young people and adults.

The problem traces back to the question of internal (organismic) and external (mechanistic) orientations, as against a humanistic view, as a way of understanding human behavior. As we suggested in Chapter 3, researchers and theorists who cannot accept a humanistic view have relied on the internal and external orientations to explain human behavior and to serve as a basis for the development of life-span research. Both the internal and external orientations assume that human lives are largely determined—that, given certain conditions, we can to a considerable extent predict what human behavior will be.

This approach, of course, will tell us much about the adult, *but it will not tell us much about the very characteristics that set us apart from other animals or from other people*. If we believe that we have the power to choose as the result of our self-awareness, then any person can choose to respond to a situation in ways that differ from those suggested in the life-span literature. The humanistic view assumes the individual to be active, not merely passive. The active person does not wait passively for the various predicted life crises to occur and then try to make the best of them. The human being has the potential to act on a situation—either to prevent it, to change it, to solve a problem, or to transcend it—as well as to accept it. The individual is not limited to accepting all the life-span changes that the research suggests will be his or her fate.

Also, there is the matter of individuality. Each person has the opportunity to react to a situation in a particular way, quite specific to that individual. Though there are often social and cultural as well as psychological forces which lead people to behave in particular ways, everyone nevertheless has a certain degree of personal freedom and choice.

Of course, we recognize that part of the life of each person *is* determined. Life is not endless. Changes do occur in the human body over time, important changes that must be recognized by all persons concerned with human life and the provision of human services. We turn, then, to a brief look at some of the changes that occur during the life span and which clearly distinguish adults from young people.

LIFE CHANGES

Someone once wrote, "The moment we began to live we began to die." Though this statement is somewhat morbid, it points to a profound truth. In common with other living matter, the human body begins, develops, deteriorates, and dies. It goes through a cycle that has been repeated throughout the aeons, a cycle that each of us is now experiencing. Though the cycle may be altered to some extent, it cannot be stopped, nor can its direction be changed.

The problem stems not from the fact that the cycle exists but from our frequent failure to accept and understand what is happening to us. Further, there is the question of how our attitude toward the cycle is allowed to affect our lives as we now live them.

Let's look at what research has shown about some of these changes. The human brain, for example, reaches its maximum weight between the ages of 20 and 30 and then declines with age. The brain's volume and the number of nerve cells also decrease with age. Research has shown that the size of the brain decreases after age 30.[9]

Some people, when they first learn what happens to their brains with age, immediately conclude that they are somehow less intelligent and thus no longer able to learn as well as children. But as Bischof says, "The brain itself is not correlated with intelligence, for idiots have been known to have brains twice the size of an average brain."[10]

And the matter of learning involves many issues beyond those of intelligence and brain size, as we will see in Chapter 12. According to research with adults, we can generalize that as humans age, they become less efficient in some respects. Again, it is easy to conclude that because one functions less efficiently as one gets older, one cannot learn as well—or, for that matter, do many other things as well as before. This line of reasoning is, of course, false. Indeed, some functions, particularly those that require physical skill and dexterity, may be less well performed as one gets older, but other skills may be performed considerably better when one is older—situations requiring experience, for example (such as decision-making situations or situations that call for good judgment).

The senses tend to grow weaker as we get older, yet they do so at different ages and different rates for different people. As we have all seen, some people do not need glasses at age 80 while others do at age 12. Yet as we look at large groups of people, research suggests that visual efficiency declines rapidly after age 40.

Likewise, one's ability to hear decreases with age: "The decrease in pitch discrimination begins about age 25, gradually decreases to about age 55, and

[9]Ledford J. Bischof, *Adult Psychology*, 2d ed., Harper & Row, New York, 1976, p. 97.
[10]Ibid., p. 97.

thereafter drops even more sharply . . . all adults hear less and less well as they age, with high frequency tones being heard less well than low tones."[11]

Reaction time tends to improve until about age 19, remains constant until about age 26, and then slowly declines from age 26 until the end of life.[12]

Of course, as we said at the outset, there are many exceptions to these declines in physical functioning. For some people, these losses occur fairly early in life; for others, much later.

INTELLIGENCE

The question of intelligence has intrigued people for a long time. It is particularly important as we look at adults. What happens to intelligence level as adults grow older? Does intelligence level decrease, remain the same, or increase?

Research has offered all three answers to the question.

The problem in any discussion of intelligence is to define what the term means as well as to create methods of testing or measuring what we've defined. One commonly accepted definition is that intelligence is what an intelligence test measures. But as Bischof says, "The concept that intelligence is what an intelligence test measures borders on intellectual dishonesty."[13]

Most people who study intelligence agree that it is not a unitary concept. Rather than having intelligence, each of us has several intelligences. Some aspects of intelligence, such as the ability to handle numbers, may be measured and quantified. But other aspects of intelligence may not be quantifiable. In this respect intelligence may be viewed in the same light as such human characteristics as humor, hope, fear, and lust. Bischof defines intelligence as "the variable capacity to solve problems of all kinds that the human is likely to encounter in life. . . . In the adult aging process social competence and effectiveness in coping are far better measures of intelligence than rearranging blocks speedily."[14]

A quality that some people relate to intelligence is *wisdom*. This is, of course, an elusive term that defies careful definition and measurement. Writers who use the term "wisdom" often suggest that it means the ability to use good judgment and discretion in relating to people and in life generally. Bischof recalls his own personal experience with wisdom and the lack of it. "My awareness arrives out of long contact with some professional co-workers who exhibited more than normal intelligence in solving professional problems, but

[11]Ibid., p. 107.
[12]Ibid., p. 143.
[13]Ibid., p. 137.
[14]Ibid., pp. 137–138.

whose conduct in life was too frequently unwise and foolish. The unfortunate result was a broken, unproductive, dismal existence."[15]

Realizing full well that intelligence cannot be reduced simply to what can be measured in an examination, let's nevertheless look at the performance of adults on such examinations.

The Wechsler Adult Intelligence Scale (WAIS) has been widely used to measure adult intelligence levels. The idea of the test is to measure whether adults "hold" or "don't hold" in several test areas. Results of research using this test suggest that adults "hold" their ability on the tests that measure vocabulary, information, and comprehension. They "don't hold" on the tests that are designed to measure object assembly, block design, and digit symbol.[16]

Jeanne G. Gilbert compared the intellectual functioning of adults aged 60 to 74 (average age 65) with their functioning when these same adults were in their twenties and early thirties. She concluded, "with the exception of vocabulary which shows a slight but insignificant increase, total group score averages and all groups of test scores show a decline over a 35-or more year period."[17]

Both the above research projects tend to show that at least in certain areas, adult intelligence decreases with age.

Other researchers have reached different conclusions. Baltes and Schaie conducted a study with 500 adults whose ages ranged from 21 to 70. They followed this group of adults over a seven-year period using Thurstone and Thurstone's Primary Mental Abilities and Schaie's Test of Behavioral Rigidity.

Baltes and Schaie, using factor-analysis methods, found that the scores on the two tests reflected four dimensions of intelligence: *crystallized intelligence* (reflects the skills one acquires from education, and from living—skills with language, with numbers, and with inductive reasoning); *cognitive flexibility* (the ability to shift one's thinking from one approach to another—such as work with antonyms and synonyms); *visualization* (organizing and processing visual materials—identifying an incomplete picture); and *visuo-motor* flexibility (the coordination of visual and motor tasks).

Baltes and Schaie discovered that crystallized intelligence and visualization scores increased dramatically with age, even for those older than 70. Cognitive flexibility remained constant. Of the four types of intelligence, only visuo-motor scores declined.

They also found in their research that generations made a difference in

[15]Ibid., p. 138.

[16]David Wechsler, *The Measurement and Appraisal of Adult Intelligence*, 5th ed., Williams & Wilkins, Baltimore, 1972.

[17]J. G. Gilbert, "Thirty-five-year Follow-up Study of Intellectual Functioning," *Journal of Gerontology*, vol. 28, no. 1, January 1973.

scores. That is, those who were born in 1906 performed less well than those born in 1913. Baltes and Schaie hypothesize that difference in performance of adults on this test is related to the educational system each generation experienced and not to declines in scores because of age.[18]

Of course, the problem with all research on adult intelligence is the one we mentioned at the very beginning of this section—a definition of intelligence. Insofar as the various tests assume various definitions of intelligence, the results also vary.

MATURITY

Many people, when asked to describe the difference between children and adults, will respond, "Children are immature, adults are supposed to be mature."

Like such words as "love," "freedom," "hope," and "dignity," "maturity" has been a difficult word for researchers to handle. Consequently, many empirical researchers avoid use of the term. Nevertheless, others find it helpful and are trying to develop a useful definition of it.

Some tend to think of maturity as a level to be achieved, a once-and-for-all, an either-or. We are either mature or immature. Bischof, on the other hand, believes that maturity is a process rather than a goal. He writes, "maturity is often easier to accept in a literary sense than in a rigorously de-fined scientific sense. As with personality, there are many kinds of maturity, many ways to express it, many avenues of conduct. Maturity is not a unitary concept."[19]

We often hear this concept discussed in terms of physical, emotional, sexual, intellectual, social, and civic maturity. If we accept these different areas of maturity, as we might surmise, some people are more mature in some areas than in others.

This brings us back to the questions raised at the beginning of this section: What is an adult? How do adults differ from children?

We could say the following:

1. Adults are more than grown-up children.
2. Adults tend to pass through several developmental stages as they move from birth to death. The adult stages, although not completely agreed upon by the life-span researchers, are clearly different from the stages experienced by young people.

[18]P. B. Baltes and K. W. Schaie, "The Myth of the Twilight Years," *Psychology Today*, Vol. 7, pp. 35–40, March 1974.

[19]Bischof, op. cit., p. 184.

3. As they age, adults experience physiological changes. Sensory functioning and reaction time decrease, for example.
4. Depending on the definition, intelligence levels in several areas may actually increase as adults grow older.
5. The quality of wisdom is often associated with adulthood, although not all adults possess it.
6. Likewise, the characteristic of maturity is often associated with adulthood, although each adult will vary concerning the level of maturity in, for example, the social, emotional, and sexual spheres.
7. Though they share similarities with other adults of the same age, adults also differ from each other and from every other human being.
8. Although faced with the inescapable prospect of aging and death, the adult human being has the potential to be conscious of what is happening and has some limited choice in modifying the process of aging. Adults also have the freedom to choose the attitude they wish to maintain toward themselves as they age.

SUMMARY

The question "What is an adult?" comes up frequently among those who work in continuing education. Many attempt to develop simplistic definitions, as, for example, "A person who is legally adult (age 18)," or "One who is economically independent from his or her parents."

Rather than attempt to develop yet another definition, we have focused our attention on *describing* the adult. We summarized some of the life-span development literature, which suggests that everyone goes through various developmental stages in the course of life. We challenged some of the deterministic assumptions that seem to support the life-span research.

We reviewed some of the research on human functions, such as changes in the brain and decreased efficiency in certain functions such as visual acuity, hearing, and reaction time.

Intelligence was explored from the perspective of how the concept relates to adults. And, though admittedly difficult to deal with, we also looked at the concepts of wisdom and maturity.

SUGGESTED READINGS

Buhler, Charlotte, and Fred Massarik (eds.): *The Course of Human Life*, Springer, New York, 1968.

Geist, Harold: *The Psychological Aspects of the Aging Process*, Warren H. Green, St. Louis, 1968.

Gould, Roger: "The Phases of Adult Life: A Study in Developmental Psychology," *American Journal of Psychiatry*, November 1972.

Goulet, L. R., and Paul B. Baltes: *Life-Span Developmental Psychology*, Academic, New York, 1970.

Kimmel, Douglas C.: *Adulthood and Aging*, Wiley, New York, 1974.

Knox, Alan B.: *Adult Development and Learning*, Jossey-Bass, San Francisco, 1977.

Long, Huey B., and Curtis Ulmer: *Are They Ever Too Old to Learn*, Prentice-Hall, Englewood Cliffs, N.J., 1971.

————and————: *The Psychology of Aging: How It Affects Learning*, Prentice-Hall, Englewood Cliffs, N.J., 1972.

————and————: *The Physiology of Aging: How It Affects Learning*, Prentice-Hall, Englewood Cliffs, N.J., 1972.

Looft, William R.: *Developmental Psychology: A Book of Readings*, Dryden, Hinsdale, Ill., 1972.

Maas, Henry S., and Joseph A. Kuyper: *From Thirty to Seventy*, Jossey-Bass, San Francisco, 1974.

Maslow, Abraham H.: *Toward A Psychology of Being*, Van Nostrand Reinhold, New York, 1968.

Montagu, Ashley: *Man in Process*, New American Library, New York, 1961.

Neugarten, Bernice L. (ed.): *Middle Age and Aging*, University of Chicago Press, Chicago, 1968.

Rose, Anthony L., and Andre Auw: *Growing Up Human*, Harper & Row, New York, 1974.

Timiras, P. S.: *Developmental Physiology*, Macmillan, New York, 1972.

SECTION III

CONTEXT FOR CONTINUING EDUCATION

The field of continuing education is sometimes described by the word "amorphous." Some see the field as a continuation of elementary, secondary, and higher education. Others prefer not to view the field this way at all but rather as something quite different from traditional schooling.

Thus there is considerable confusion. In Chapter 5 we discuss the problems of describing and labeling the field of continuing education. We argue the importance of taking a comprehensive view. And rather than suggest one more definition of continuing education, we offer a description of the field from the perspective of audience, agencies, and providers and its potential for self-directedness. Last, we explore the problems with labeling.

In Chapter 6 we outline the many problems the field faces in determining its purposes. Among these is the fact that much of adult education seems to be dominated by an "either-or" mentality—developmentalist versus rationalist, individuals versus society, or vocational versus liberal education.

Then, in Chapter 7, we present a rationale for purposes. We suggest that the purposes of continuing education should be (1) to help people survive, (2) to help people discover a sense of meaning, (3) to help people learn how to learn, and (4) to help communities (society) provide a more humane environment for their members.

CHAPTER 5

Problems in Describing and Labeling the Field

A few years ago I was asked to speak to the National Advisory Council on Adult Education in Washington. I was chairing the Commission of Professors of Adult Education at the time and the advisory council was seeking several perspectives on the field, including what the professors were thinking about.

In preparation for that talk, I reflected back on some of my experiences in the field, read several of the documents the Commission of Professors had recently prepared, and talked to several of my fellow professors about what they thought I might share with the advisory council.

I recall vividly the day I spoke to the group. It was pouring rain in Washington and my plane was more than an hour late. The executive director of the Adult Education Association—USA met me at the airport and hustled me off to the downtown hotel where I was to meet with the council. I arrived at the meeting with only minutes to spare.

I was introduced to the group by the chairman and I proceeded to share the remarks that I thought were representative of where the field of adult education was and where it ought to be going in the next few years. The group listened attentively. But I sensed something was wrong. At the conclusion of my half-hour talk, two people asked polite questions but no one commented or asked questions about what I considered to be the more important parts of my presentation.

Back at the airport later that afternoon, the rain still streaming down the terminal windows, I sat and pondered what had gone wrong. I didn't feel good about the meeting. Why was the response so guarded? Could my personal politics be wrong? But how could the group know my politics? Had I made some serious error in my presentation that they were too polite to call to my attention? Did they really not think much about professors of adult education, and had they called me to Washington merely to meet some requirement that all sides be heard?

I pondered all these questions and more on the flight back to Madison. I didn't have the answer to my concern until I returned to my office and looked up some more information about the advisory council. As I carefully read its objectives, I discovered, to my embarrassment, that they were concerned only with matters related to adult basic education, not to the broad field concerned with the education of all adults. I had spoken broadly in my comments, *including* adult basic education but certainly not limiting my comments to this segment of the field.

That was not the first time I ran into the labeling problem faced by those of us concerned with the education of adults. In this instance, I was using the label "adult education" to mean the entire field. The advisory council was using the same label to mean one specific part of the field.

To show you how complicated the problem is, I have, during the past few months, kept a list of the labels I have found in the literature and heard in talks given by educators of adults. The labels I have listed include "lifelong education," "lifelong learning," "continuous learning," "continuous education," "continuing education," "adult education," "adult learning," "permanent education" (or the French *éducation permanent*), "postsecondary education," "recurrent education," "informal education," "nonformal study," "andragogy," and "nontraditional study." I'm sure many of the readers of this book could add to the list. Some people use these terms interchangeably, while others attach specific meanings to them.

Although these labels are generally used to refer broadly to the field, there is another list of labels used to connote specific parts of the field. Some of these more specific labels are "adult basic education," "secondary education for adults," "training and development," "public school adult education," "adult vocational and technical education," "liberal adult education," "extension education," "community development," "cooperative extension," "agricultural extension," "community education," "community school education," "career education," "adult performance-level education," "in-service training," "nondirected education," "self-directed education," "self-directed learning," "nonschool education," "on-the-job education," "distance education," "higher adult education," "continuing professional education," "advanced education." Again, you probably would not find it difficult to add to this list.

The point of all of this is that we have an abundance of labels designating the education of adults. And the labels are not all commonly understood. Some people use the same term to refer to different aspects of the field, while others use different terms to refer to the same aspect.

To begin to sort out this problem of labeling, we must first spend some time understanding that which we are trying to label. If we can't agree on what something is, then we surely can't agree on what its label should be.

In this chapter, we will explore the need to describe the field and look at some of the problems associated with describing it. Once we have done this, we will consider ways to make sense of the labeling problem.

THE NEED FOR DESCRIPTION

It would seem only logical to begin by asking: What is this field that is concerned with the education of adults?

But not all would agree that it is necessary to try to understand the field, to try in some way to set limits around it, to be able to say with some degree of confidence what it is and what it is not. Any attempt to describe or give structure to the field will narrow and exclude, these critics of description argue. They point out that the field is still so young that one cannot yet know what should be included in it and what should be excluded. To define parameters too soon, they say, may destroy some of the more creative dimensions of the field, some of which haven't as yet been developed.

Also, these critics of description and delineation argue that along with description comes a progression of steps that will make the field narrower and more specialized. The field will become the same as primary, secondary, and higher education, with their well-defined sets of rules concerning what the curriculum is, who is certified to teach, and what constitutes a credential for those who complete various courses of study. Nevertheless, there are some compelling reasons why we should attempt to get a better grasp of what this field concerned with the education of adults is all about.

The Need to Gain Support

Though the number of adults participating in various kinds of educational activities is at an all-time high, the field continues to be marginal in terms of the support it receives from decision makers at every level. When someone speaks about the need for tax dollars to support some phase of secondary education, they know, generally, what secondary education is about. But when someone speaks about tax dollars to support some phase of the education of adults, there is not only lack of understanding about the field but also lack of agreement on the label to be used.

Along with support from decision makers must come general support from the public. Decision makers, particularly those who are concerned with tax dollars, must have public support or at least understanding on the part of the public. Some segments of the public are excited by the prospect of the education of adults, but we are far from having achieved a broad understanding of the field.

Development of a Body of Knowledge

Across the country, degree programs are offered at the undergraduate and graduate levels for those who want to pursue careers in adult education. Those who are responsible for the development of such courses of study are obviously keenly interested in how the field is described, for such description guides them in the selection of materials for courses and other learning experiences for the degree programs.

Directly related is research in the field. If any field is to grow and develop, research must take place. But—on a very practical level—if we aren't able to describe the field to be researched, it is difficult to know what to research.

What has happened, in many instances, is that researchers from the perspectives of sociology, psychology, political science, or some other field of study have looked at the education of adults from the viewpoint of their fields and then communicated this information to people working with the education of adults. Or, those working with adult education have gone to the various other fields of study and looked for research that seems to apply to the education of adults.

Robert D. Boyd and I have pointed out some of the difficulties that ensue when this strategy is followed. We note that the other disciplines such as sociology or psychology did not have the education of adults in mind when they developed concepts. And if we accept the idea, as this book maintains, that the education of adults is a field of study unlike other fields, then we must be cautious about borrowing concepts from other fields. A concept, as Boyd and I argue, is developed within a particular context. A concept developed within some sociological context, for example, may or may not be applicable to the field concerned with the education of adults.

Of course the implication, in the long run, of borrowing concepts from other fields is that these other fields then are responsible for defining what the education of adults is all about.[1] Do we want other fields to define what our field should be?

---

[1]Robert D. Boyd and Jerold W. Apps, *A Conceptual Model for Adult Education*, unpublished manuscript, Department of Continuing and Vocational Education, University of Wisconsin—Madison, Madison, Wis., 1977.

The Need for a Comprehensive View of the Field

A practical reason for attempting to describe the field more carefully is to help those who now work in it to see it more broadly. Here it will help to use another analogy. Think of a forest that includes oak, maple, elm, hickory, aspen, birch, and several other species of trees. If we were to walk into that forest and, with a magnifying glass, inspect a birch tree carefully, we would learn some very interesting things. If we were to do this each day for many days, we would likely become quite expert about birch trees. And with our intense interest in birch trees, we would likely pay little or no attention to oaks or any of the other trees in the forest.

Such is the case with many persons who now work in some activity concerned with the education of adults. They know a great deal about the aspect of the field in which they work, but they know little about "the other trees in the forest."

As we are pointing out here, this problem is not entirely the fault of those working in the field. The attempts made to describe the forest with all its trees haven't been all that successful in helping people to understand what the field is about.

To push the analogy a little further, attempts have been made to help people understand something about the various trees—public school adult education, extension education, vocational adult education—but not about the forest as a whole. We argue that the forest—continuing education as a whole—is more than the sum of the agencies, institutions, and what have you that make it up. In short, many people really *can't* see the forest for the trees. Many people can't see the big picture because of their exclusive focus on special aspects of it.

We start then, with the critical necessity of attempting to achieve better understanding of this field concerned with adults and education. Though we recognize the problems associated with carrying this exercise too far, as outlined earlier in this section, we also recognize the compelling reasons for dealing with the problem.

PROBLEMS WITH DESCRIPTION

We begin by dealing with some underlying problems, attempting to differentiate between education and learning and between education and schooling.

Education and Learning

A good deal of confusion exists in the literature between the terms education and learning. Sometimes they are used to mean the same thing, other times they are used to describe quite different phenomena.

For our discussion here, I would like to separate the two terms and consider them as quite distinct though related.

Learning is an activity of the person who learns. It may involve acquiring information or skills. It may involve reorganization of presently held ideas. It may involve acquisition of new attitudes, new feelings, or changes in values. Learning often results in changed behavior, and it can lead people to grow toward reaching their potentials. In summary, learning involves change.[2]

Random Learning   Learning may be random or it may be planned. This is an extremely important concept. All of us, as we live our lives, learn a great many things randomly. When we walk to work, carry out the garbage, ride on the bus, scan the morning headlines and watch the television news, we learn. We learn a great deal this way, often not being aware that we are learning.

Some of the most profound things we have learned were not planned but simply happened. A child who for the first time discovers a wildflower in a quiet forest has learned something of beauty, of relationship, and of discovery itself. When we sit together, as a group of friends, around a campfire listening to the snapping and crackling fire and the sounds of the night, we can learn.

When we sit with a good novel intending only to entertain ourselves but then discover that the message, though subtle and heavy with metaphor, has given us insight into our lives, we have learned.

When we listen to good music and find that the notes strike at our emotions so vividly that tears stream down our cheeks and we discover new feelings, we are learning.

At first glance, random learning appears insignificant compared to all the planned learning made available through our various institutions and agencies. Yet with some reflection on our own learning, we quickly discover how profound and important much of our random learning has been.

Planned Learning   Planned, or deliberate, learning is that learning which we deliberately set out to do. We as learners may do the planning for this learning or others may plan it for us.

Here is where we link learning to education. *Education may be defined as organized and planned activity with the intent that learning will result. This activity may be available to individuals, groups, or communities.*

Often associated with a definition of education is the term "educational system." An educational system is defined as the combination of institutions,

[2]See Chapter 12 for a more in-depth discussion of learning.

agencies, organizations, and facilities that have as one of their purposes providing such organized and planned activity whose purpose is learning.

What are the categories that make up an educational system? We can categorize institutions, agencies, organizations, and facilities in two ways: (1) by their degree of formality or informality and (2) by their degree of involvement with the education of adults.

"Formal," in this sense, refers to those institutions or agencies that offer credits, degrees, or other credentials and have a planned curriculum with emphasis on the cumulation of educational experiences. Included here are college and university degree programs.

Informal educational opportunities generally include little or no emphasis on credentials, may not emphasize the accumulation of educational experiences, and frequently have few if any requirements for prior achievement before a person may participate.

In terms of their degree of involvement with adults, institutions vary:

Some, such as the Cooperative Extension Service and adult basic education programs, operate primarily for the education of adults.

Others have educational purposes, but the education of adults is of secondary importance; an example is public school adult education.

Still others—such as libraries, museums, art centers and the like—include the education of adults among their broad purposes.

Finally, there are those institutions whose primary purposes are not educational but which often include the education of adults as one aspect of their activity; examples are community development organizations, civic organizations, labor unions, business and industry, government, mass media, welfare, and medical services.

The problem with our description of the educational system as we have developed it so far is that it is external to the learner. Reflecting on what we have just said, it could be concluded that an educational system is made up of institutions, agencies, organizations, and facilities doing something—intervening—in the lives of adults, who often have little to say about the matter.

Indeed this is one of the hottest issues in the field today—that of compulsory continuing education. One position is that certain groups of adults, such as those in life-saving professions, *must* participate in specified educational opportunities in order to maintain their credentials. This is usually translated to mean those opportunities that are provided by certain institutions where credentials, credits, and so on are made available for time (and money) spent on learning.

Others strongly oppose the concept of compulsory continuing education and argue that it strikes at the very autonomy of human beings, forcing them to be the targets of, and dependent on, educational providers. Our purpose is not to get into the issue of compulsory continuing education at this time but to show that any definition of education must consider the autonomy of indivudual learners.

We have a dilemma. We could say, as some have, that all schools should be abolished because they violate the autonomv of individuals, teach people to be dependent, to follow orders, stand in lines, and generally to become pawns of a growing military-industrial complex that is slowly taking over the country.[3]

Rather than advocate the abolishment of all institutions concerned for the education of adults, let's attempt to transcend this conflict between individuals seeking autonomy versus institutions attempting to intervene in their lives by suggesting that learners be included as central to the educational system. That is, especially as we consider *adult* education, let us include the concept of self-directed learning as one important part of a definition of education.

What does including the learner as a part of the educational system really mean? It means that we are committed to the idea that learners should be responsible for their own learning and for their own education—the opportunities they wish to pursue in order to learn. At times the learner will select books from the library, perhaps talk with some friends, maybe interview some "expert" to obtain answers to a question or solve a problem. At other times the learner, who may be planning a career change, may recognize the need to enroll in a degree program at a university where much of the planning has already been done. But it is up to the learner to decide what route will be taken. The learner, aware of the many options and the many elements of an educational system, chooses and selects throughout his or her life depending on where that learner happens to be in terms of learning needs.

It is easy, as we talk about an educational system, to exclude the learner as we become concerned about budgets, staffing, and all the other problems involved in keeping a system alive and well. But we must constantly be reminded that the system is to serve the people, not the other way around. It is also easy to exclude society as we talk about educational systems. Educational systems should serve not only the needs of individuals but also those of society. It is commonly accepted that educational institutions have responsibility for providing training for the variety of tasks and functions necessary to society as a whole.

[3]See Ivan Illich, *Deschooling Society*, Harper & Row, New York, 1971, and Everett Reimer, *School is Dead: Alternatives in Education*, Doubleday, New York, 1971.

Education and Schooling

By now it should be evident that in our definition of education, schooling makes up only one element. Yet it is common across the country today to equate schooling and education as if they were one and the same. Particularly as we think about the education of adults, we must realize that much of adult education occurs outside formal classrooms.

A LOOK AT DEFINITIONS

One way of attempting to answer the question of what continuing education is is to search for definitions. It is not difficult to find them. For instance, in the spring 1955 issue of *Adult Leadership*, some fourteen pages were devoted to an article titled "What is Adult Education? Nine Working Definitions."

Let's look at a few of the definitions offered by the literature of recent years. To begin with: "Adult education is synonymous with 'out-of-school education' and means organized programs of education provided for the benefit of and adapted to the needs of persons not in regular school and university system and generally fifteen or over."[4]

Stanley Sworder defined the field this way: "In looking at this matter of a working definition of adult education, I see it as an educational program that is planned and organized to assist adults in meeting their responsibilities as individuals and as members of society."[5]

In the same publication, Carl Minich wrote, "I conceive adult education to be a continuing educational experience which should contribute to the growth of people as long as they live."[6]

Lawrence K. Frank perceived adult education this way:

Adult education may be regarded as a social invention peculiarly appropriate to our times, offering ways whereby adults can be helped to recognize the necessity for these large scale changes and to undertake the laborious task of examining, clarifying, and deciding the ways in which they will, as adults, accept the responsibility for renewing our culture and reorienting our social order.[7]

---

[4]Definition provided by the 1975 handbook *International Standard Classification of Education* and quoted in James R. Broschart, *Lifelong Learning in the Nation's Third Century*, Office of Education, Washington, D.C., 1977, p. 11.

[5]Stanley Sworder, "What is Adult Education? Nine 'Working Definitions,'" *Adult Education*, vol. 5, pp. 131–145, Spring 1955.

[6]Ibid.

[7]Ibid.

Coolie Verner wrote:

Adult education is a relationship between an educational agent and a learner in which the agent selects, arranges, and continuously directs a sequence of progressive tasks that provide systematic experience to achieve learning for people whose participation in such activities is subsidiary and supplemental to a primary productive role in society.[8]

Despite the problem of different labels, it is useful to include some definitions of the field concerned with the education of adults using labels other than "adult education." For example, in the 1977 revisions of the 1965 Higher Education Act, "lifelong learning" is defined as follows:

Lifelong learning includes, but is not limited to, adult basic education, continuing education, independent study, agricultural education, business education and labor education, occupational education and job training programs, parent education, postsecondary education, preretirement and education for older and retired people, remedial education, special education programs for groups or for individuals with special needs, and also educational activities designed to upgrade occupational and professional skills, to assist business, public agencies, and other organizations in the use of innovation and research results, and to serve family needs and personal development.[9]

The Accrediting Commission of the Continuing Education Council defines "continuing education" as

. . . the further development of human abilities after entrance into employment or voluntary activities. It includes in-service, upgrading and updating education. It may be occupational education or training which furthers career or personal development. Continuing Education includes that study made necessary by advances in knowledge. It excludes most general education and training for job entry. Continuing education is concerned primarily with broad personal and professional development. It includes leadership training and the improvement of the ability to manage personal, financial, material and human resources. Most of the

[8]Coolie Verner, "Definition of Terms," in Gale Jensen, A. A. Liveright, and Wilbur Hallenbeck (eds.), *Adult Education: Outlines of an Emerging Field of University Study*, Adult Education Association of the USA, Washington, D.C., 1964, pp. 30–32.

[9]*Congressional Record*, Higher Education Act, 1965, P. L. 89.329, 1977 revisions, Section 132, Lifelong Learning.

subject matter is at the professional, technical and leadership training levels or the equivalent.[10]

Harrington defines adult education this way: "adult education refers to those who have completed or interrupted their schooling and are entering a college or university or are coming into contact with higher education after an interval away from the classroom." He says this about continuing education: "[it is] often used as a synonym for adult education, [but] will here be limited to those who are building on previous training."[11]

What have we learned from all this? It's obvious that there is no one definition that refers to the *field* concerned with the education of adults. Some of the definitions emphasize the component parts of the field. Other definitions emphasize the adult learner and what benefits he or she may obtain from participation. From reading the definitions, we can see quickly that labels and their use can get in the way of a clear understanding of the field. Harrington, for example, speaks of adult education in terms of the role of colleges and universities. Most of the others use a much broader definition of adult education. All the definitions focus on the individual learner. None of them defines the field to include groups, communities, and institutions as suitable participants and benefactors for what the field has to offer.

By now we have probably made this field, concerned with the education of adults, seem elusive, ambiguous, contradictory, and perplexing. Rather than attempt another definition to add to the collection, let us be more modest in our efforts. Let's attempt to describe the field as an approach to understanding.

A DESCRIPTION OF THE FIELD

As we suggested above, by attempting to define the field we run the risk either of excluding some important component that now exists or may exist in the future, on the one hand, and, on the other, be so broad and general that our definition serves little useful purpose.

By attempting to describe various dimensions of the field we are able to provide some understanding and perhaps at the same time avoid some of the problems associated with definition.

Below we will explore the dimensions of (1) multiple audiences, (2) multiple agencies and providers, and (3) self-directed potential.

[10]Continuing Education Council, *The Benefits of Being Accredited by the Continuing Education Council*, Continuing Education Council, Homer Kempfer, Executive Director, Richmond, Va. (no date).

[11]Fred Harvey Harrington, *The Future of Adult Education*: *New Responsibilities of Colleges and Universities*, Jossey-Bass, San Francisco, 1977, p. xii.

Multiple Audiences for the Field

One dimension of the field that confuses many people and often leads to problems with labeling is the diversity of audiences involved. Several audiences can be identified:

1. *People with basic and secondary educational needs.* This includes the clients of adult basic education programs. They often lack functional literacy, high school equivalency, or the skills necessary for coping with daily life.

2. *People who need occupational and vocational training.* Here we include those who lack sufficient skills to obtain a job, those who wish to upgrade occupational competencies, and those who wish to obtain new skills and knowledge so they can change jobs. It also includes the large numbers of adults who have been employed and are now returning to colleges, vocational-technical schools, and universities in order to prepare for a career shift. Finally, it includes large numbers of women who are entering the work force for the first time or who are returning after their children have grown.

3. *Professionals who need to upgrade their knowledge and skills constantly.* Here we include professionals in health, law, teaching, engineering, business, and other areas who constantly feel the need to upgrade their professional skills and knowledge. It is with this group that the present controversy over compulsory continuing education rests. Should certain professionals be forced to participate in continuing education activities in order to be certified and to remain in good standing in their respective fields?

4. *Adults seeking self-enrichment/liberal education/leisure-time skills.* This audience includes thousands of adults who are participating in short courses, workshops, self-study programs, media-sponsored activities, and a host of other offerings, all designed to help the individual to improve in some way. Included in this group are people who wish to improve the quality of their lives through the study of classical literature, music, and art and those who wish to develop some personal talent such as creative writing, painting, or a performing art.

5. *Adults who seek skills and knowledge in community and social action.* Increasing numbers of adults are becoming involved in community decision making and problem solving, yet they often lack the necessary skills for such activity. Seminars, short courses, and workshops can help to provide these skills.

6. *Groups and communities in which citizens live.* An important point is that groups and communities as well as individuals have needs. A group or community need is not necessarily the same as the sum of the needs of those who make up that group or community. Groups and communities are entities different from and greater than the sum of the individuals who belong to them. Sometimes this issue is defined as the relationship between societal and

individual needs. Rather than use the broader term "society," we prefer the concepts of small groups and communities.

Multiple Agencies and Providers

Once again we wish to emphasize that schooling, as we shall see below, is but one of many agencies that provide educational opportunities for adults. Thus it is limiting to thinking about the education of adults as a fourth category of schooling in addition to those of elementary, secondary, and higher education. Continuing education includes schooling, but it is much broader and more comprehensive.

1. *Mass media.* Though little is yet known about the effectiveness of the mass media as an educational agency for adults, no one would doubt that millions of people are participating. It is particularly difficult to determine the extent to which adults are participating in organized educational activities provided by the mass media. Without question, the mass media contribute greatly to the random learning that we all experience. But the question is: How much contribution is made to education as we have defined it?

2. *Employers and work settings.* Most businesses and industries have educational programs of one type or another for their employees. They may be of an in-service nature, designed to help employees cope with a new machine, for example. Or they may be designed to promote self-improvement, including educational opportunities with a cultural orientation. Government, including the military, also has extensive educational programming.

3. *Proprietary schools.* Privately operated, these schools offer both correspondence and on-site instruction. Topics offered range from diesel truck driving to typewriting, from how to invest in the stock market to creative writing.

4. *Higher education.* Colleges and universities are increasingly reviewing their traditional degree programs to make them more available to adults returning to school for either first or advanced degrees. Across the country, there is a trend for large numbers of adults who have been away from formal study for many years to return either to begin a college program, finish a degree they once started and didn't complete, or work toward an advanced degree.

Colleges, community colleges, and universities are also increasingly offering noncredit courses in a host of subject-matter areas for adult audiences. Many institutions of higher education have substantial outreach offices that concentrate their efforts on programming for adult audiences. Many have also opened continuing education counseling centers for adults who are contemplating a return to college, either for degree or nondegree work, and want to know how to do it. Often these people lack study skills and confidence in returning to formal study, whatever the form it may take.

5. *Cooperative extension.* Beginning in 1914, with the passage of the

Smith-Lever Act, this institution has become the largest of its type in the world. It combines the contributions of three governmental levels: the U.S. Department of Agriculture, the land-grant university in each state, and county government. Its professional people usually reside at the county seat in each state. They are responsible for developing programs with local citizens in such areas as agriculture, land-use planning, environmental concerns, family living, and youth development through 4-H programs. In recent years, cooperative extension has increasingly moved into the rural nonfarm and urban areas with programming. A strong feature of the program is grass roots planning with professionals who work in local areas tied to a research-knowledge base at the land-grant university.

6. *Public schools.* Increasingly, public schools are used as a community resource center, with programs directed to adults of all ages. Some emphasis has recently been directed toward retired and elderly persons living in the community. Many public schools also conduct programs in adult basic education for citizens living in the community.

7. *Other agencies as providers of adult education opportunities.* Here we include such agencies as libraries, museums, park and recreation centers; churches and religious organizations; community service and action programs; health and welfare agencies; the YWCA and YMCA; philanthropic agencies; organizations of senior citizens; service clubs such as the Lions, the Kiwanis, and the Rotary; political parties; citizen organizations such as women's organizations; and more. Many of these offer educational programs in one form or another for adults.[12]

Continuing Education May be Self-Directed

As mentioned earlier, one important characteristic of the education of adults is that it may be self-directed, either in whole or in part. It is easy to lose sight of this concept when we review the many educational offerings for adults that are available in our society. But we must constantly be reminded that any total description of education for adults must include the concept of self-direction. Allen Tough has done considerable research in this area. His findings indicate that some 70 percent of the learning projects participated in by adults are the type that are self-directed.[13] This is an amazing figure considering that we sometimes assume, erroneously, that all education is planned and directed by some educational institution.

The field of continuing education is turning increasingly to the concept of

[12]Some of this material is adapted from James R. Broschart, *Lifelong Learning in the Nation's Third Century*, U.S. Office of Education, Washington, D.C., 1977, p. 46.

[13]Allen Tough, *The Adult's Learning Projects*, Ontario Institute for Studies in Education, Toronto, 1971, p. 1.

self-directed education. Malcolm Knowles has developed a strategy that the self-directed adult might follow in planning for learning.[14]

Ronald Gross, in *The Lifelong Learner*, discusses the concepts of self-directed learning and the advantages to be obtained by those who attempt to follow the idea. He also shares several case studies of "lifelong learners in action."[15]

And in a book I prepared for those adults who are returning to formal study in a college, vocational-technical school, or university, I have outlined an approach designed to help such students to organize self-directed efforts.[16]

DECIDING ON A LABEL—"CONTINUING EDUCATION"

Now that we have attempted an outline description of the field, it is time to come back to the problem of labels. We could, of course, simply dismiss the problem and accept the fact there are and will probably continue to be many labels to describe the education of adults. But, as we argued earlier in this chapter, if the field is ever to achieve identity—which is necessary to garner support from decision makers and understanding from the public—we believe that we must agree on a label. But just as there are dangers in attempting to write a definition for the education of adults, there are also dangers in attempting to select a label.

We must be careful to choose a label that is sufficiently comprehensive to describe the totality of the field and is not limited to some segment of it. The label should also be one that could include dimensions of the field that have not yet been described or explored. The label should be, on the other hand, sufficiently descriptive that it clearly refers to the field and is not confused with other endeavors, either educational or otherwise. The label should not confuse the parts of the field, the components that make it up, with the totality of the field. Finally, the label chosen should reflect the differences between education and learning, as we discussed earlier in this chapter.

Historically, the two labels that have been used most often in describing the field have been "continuing education" and "adult education." Given the criteria listed above, our preference is for the label "continuing education." Why have we not chosen to emphasize "adult education" as the label, given that the literature uses this label considerably more often? There are several practical reasons for this decision.

1. For many people, "adult education" connotes "catching up." This has been reaffirmed with the development of adult basic education programs that

[14]Malcolm Knowles, *Self-Directed Learning*, Association Press, New York, 1975.

[15]Ronald Gross, *The Lifelong Learner*, Simon and Schuster, New York, 1977.

[16]Jerold W. Apps, *Study Skills: For Those Adults Returning to School*, McGraw-Hill, New York, 1978.

do emphasize this aspect of learning. It is further affirmed with the language training that is being offered to large numbers of people for whom English is a second language. Unfortunately, these "catching up" programs are commonly referred to as "adult education." For many people, this is the beginning and the end of what the field is about.

2. Much of the national legislation, and state legislation as well, uses the label "adult education" to mean adult basic education. Recently, I was reading a very attractive report on adult education prepared by a state department of education. The entire report was concerned with adult basic education, its programming, successes, and challenges. Not once did the report recognize that the education of adults *includes* basic education but is far broader than that.

3. As we pointed out previously, there is the continuing and vexing problem of defining the word "adult." Furthermore, in the minds of many, the word "adult" suggests a singular set of characteristics and needs. The implication is that all adults are similar and that therefore their educational needs are similar. This is obviously false. By using the term "adult education" we risk perpetuating the myth of the sameness of adults.

4. Adult education is easily construed to be a fourth category of education, to take its place alongside primary, secondary, and higher education. Although there are some people working in the field who would agree that this is the correct assessment, there are many others who would strongly resist any attempt to define the field as a fourth category of the recognized institutions of education.

Ohliger, quoting an unnamed professor of education, writes that continuing education "cannot become a viable alternative to a decadent educational system when those in it see it only as an extension of that system, rather than a unique opportunity to create a new learning alternative."[17]

5. From the standpoint of good English, the label "adult education" presents a problem. In a conversation with a friend who is a professor of psychology, I used the term "adult educator." His response was, "Well, I should *hope* these educators you talk about are adults." He has a point. We don't label those teaching children as "child educators." We haven't solved the problem of a label for the professional by using "continuing education" either. How can we use the related term "continuing educator" without causing some confusion and perhaps some snickers? I can hear my friend asking, "Do you mean educators that just go on forever?"

I attempt to solve this problem by using the term "educator of adults," realizing that it is clumsy and also has potential problems. But it has fewer problems than either "adult educator" or "continuing educator."

[17]John Ohliger, "Prospects for a Learning Society," *Adult Leadership*, vol. 24, no. 1, pp. 37–40, September 1975.

Before we leave the problem of labeling, I'd like to mention two related problems. There are those in the field who have attempted to promote the use of new labels. Thus some speak about "andragogy," a term developed in Europe and promoted in this country by Malcolm Knowles.[18]

We also have people constantly searching for and promoting labels that smack of faddism. "Lifelong learning" has become a term that is in vogue at this writing. Another is "nontraditional study," which in some quarters is defined as any kind of opportunity offered by a college or university to those over 25.

"Distance education" is another term that has been used to describe one type of correspondence study. Still another is "schools without walls."

These terms may have a place in the development of the field of continuing education, for they become catch phrases around which to rally public support. But we must be careful to keep our terms in tune with and related to some overall, agreed-upon label so that we don't constantly confuse the public and the decision makers instead of gaining their support.

SUMMARY

Anyone beginning to look at the field of continuing education immediately discovers a host of labels such as "adult education," "lifelong learning," "continuous learning," and "recurrent education," to mention a few. Some of these labels are used synonymously, others are used to describe specific aspects of continuing education, such as education for adults lacking basic skills and education for professionals seeking to upgrade their skills and competencies.

Although there is no lack of definitions, the definitions often disagree. Thus one who is attempting to become acquainted with the field is quickly confused and often bewildered.

In this chapter we have argued for the need to describe the field more carefully. The reasons offered are (1) the need to gain support for the field, (2) the difficulty of developing research and a subsequent body of knowledge without a clearer sense of what constitutes the field, and (3) to help those working in the field who don't really understand its scope.

The problems of differentiating between education and learning and between education and schooling were discussed. Several definitions, developed by many people over the years, were presented.

Rather than attempt to offer yet another definition, we provided an overall description of the field. The following were suggested as components of the field: (1) multiple audiences, (2) multiple agencies and providers, and (3) self-directed potential.

[18]Malcolm Knowles, *The Modern Practice of Adult Education: Andragogy versus Pedagogy*, Association Press, New York, 1970.

"Adult education" and "continuing education" are the two general labels most commonly used for the field. Several reasons were suggested why the term "adult education" causes difficulties when it is used as a general label. Thus we prefer "continuing education" as the label most applicable for the field.

SUGGESTED READINGS

Bergevin, Paul: *A Philosophy for Adult Education*, Seabury, New York, 1967.

Blakely, Robert J.: "What is Adult Education?" in Malcolm S. Knowles (ed.), *Handbook of Adult Education in the United States*, Adult Education Association of the USA, Chicago, 1960.

Boyd, Robert D.: "Psychological Definition of Adult Education," *Adult Leadership*, vol. 15, pp. 160–162, November 1966.

Cremin, Lawrence: *Traditions of American Education*, Basic Books, New York, 1977.

Dickerman, Watson: "What is this 'Continuing Education'?" *Adult Education*, vol. 15, pp. 3–9, Autumn 1964.

Godbey, G. C.: "After All, What is Adult Education?" *Adult Leadership*, vol. 15, p. 165, November 1966.

Houle, Cyril: *The Design of Education*, Jossey-Bass, San Francisco, 1972.

Klevins, Chester (ed.): *Materials and Methods in Continuing Education*, Klevins Publications, Los Angeles, 1976.

Lengrand, Paul: *An Introduction to Lifelong Education*, Croom Helm, London, 1975.

Mead, Margaret: "A Redefinition of Education," *NEA Journal*, vol. 48, pp. 15–17, October 1959.

Schroeder, Wayne: "Adult Education Defined and Described," in Robert M. Smith, George F. Aker, and J. R. Kidd (eds.), *Handbook of Adult Education*, Macmillan, New York, 1970.

Verner, Coolie: *A Conceptual Scheme for the Identification and Classification of Processes for Adult Education*, Adult Education Association of the USA, Chicago, 1962.

CHAPTER 6

Problems in Defining Purposes

Just as there is confusion and a diversity of views about how continuing education should be defined and labeled, there is also confusion about its purpose. On the surface, the problem is a simple one and quite easily solved. What is the purpose of continuing education? Why, it's the education of adults. Too often, however, we allow that answer to stand without exploring what is meant by the words "the education of adults."

As we begin to look at the problem, we quickly realize how complex it is. Before we even begin to analyze it, we note that many educators of adults don't see the question of purpose as a problem.

> *Most adult education practitioners are content to see adult education as a patternless mosaic of pluralistic aims. . . . If pressed to give a rationale for this tolerance of chaos they are likely to say something about it being the democratic way. They will declare their faith in the individual's right and ability to choose what will be in his and society's greatest interest, given full information and free choice.*[1]

[1]Malcolm S. Knowles, "Philosophical Issues that Confront Adult Educators," *Adult Education*, vol. 7, no. 4, Summer 1957.

For several practical reasons, however, increasing numbers of continuing education professionals recognize the need to wrestle with the question of purpose.

1. An understanding of the purpose of continuing education will enhance an overall understanding of the field, both for those who work in the field and for those whose support it requires.

2. Clearly understood purposes will help all those associated with the field—and this includes nearly every adult—have some sense of what might be attained through continuing education. This sense of *attainment* will also serve as a guide for the selection of processes that might most appropriately be used. Thus understanding of purpose will help people know what they can expect from participating in continuing education compared with what they might expect from the activities of other human services such as the health professions and the religious community. Obviously, continuing education cannot do everything in a community, but what can it reasonably be expected to do?

3. By knowing what are appropriate purposes for continuing education, it is possible from time to time for a community to reflect on whether or not those purposes are being attained. In other words, clear purposes provide a means of evaluation.

In this chapter we will analyze purposes for continuing education as they now exist. In Chapter 7, we will develop a rationale for what the purposes should be.

As we review the writings in continuing education, we discover that purposes are often dichotomized. That is, they are often described in terms of either/or categories. We will begin our analysis by exploring several of these dichotomies.

DEVELOPMENTALIST VERSUS RATIONALIST

Powell and Benne argue that all of continuing education is polarized between the opposing purposes referred to as developmentalist and rationalist. Those who subscribe to the developmentalist school see the purpose of continuing education to be that of development, either of communities or of individuals. Traditionally the developmentalist school of thought has been represented by those educators of adults who are a part of the community development movement and those who are concerned with human relations, encounter groups, and the like.

In recent years, considerable emphasis has been placed on the concept of *learning how to learn*. This concept is an example of the developmentalist approach, for it emphasizes helping people to learn the process of learning and, as a result, to become autonomous learners. The developmentalists are also problem-oriented, beginning with a problem and then attempting to solve it.

The rationalist school operates under such labels as "liberal arts," "reading-discussion," "great books," and the humanities. The emphasis is on content, "but the goal has shifted from the acquisition of knowledge to the sharpening of judgment, and from scholarship as such to an understanding of ideas and values in relation to social and personal goals in living."[2]

Some people would include under the rationalist label those who see the purpose of continuing education as *passing on the culture*. These people argue that over the centuries humanity has discovered, collected, and stored vast amounts of knowledge, and that the fundamental purpose of education is to transmit this knowledge from one generation to the next. Ideally, these people argue, this transmission should be achieved through the teaching of children. But if for one reason or another the transmission were incomplete, then it would become a purpose of continuing education to complete the process. Also, with the discovery of new knowledge, it is impossible for people to complete their educations when they are young. As it is discovered, knowledge must continually be transmitted to everyone.

The content-process dichotomy represents one of the important differences between the rationalist and developmentalist orientations. Although both the developmentalists and the rationalists obviously stress content to some degree, the rationalists begin with content, whereas the developmentalists begin with a situation or problem. Content, for the developmentalist, is significant as a part of the process of dealing with a problem only if it has direct application to the problem. The rationalist school of thought, on the other hand, is interested in process, but only insofar as process is of use in helping to promote the acquisition of content.

Both approaches, the rationalist and the developmentalist, agree on the individual as the learner in contrast with those who accept the group and the community as participants in educational efforts.

Powell and Benne argue that

... "individual and group," "individual and society," are false dichotomies, since neither exists without the other and they must be defined in terms of each other. ... It is the individual adult who is trying to "find himself" in the fluid society from which he is so easily alienated; to "relate himself" to his fellows; to "express himself" in the arts, or "assert himself" in civic action; and in all the shared uses of his mind upon his memberships and relationships to "become visible to himself," self-creative.[3]

[2]John Walker Powell and Kenneth D. Benne, "Philosophies of Adult Education," in Malcolm S. Knowles (ed.), *Handbook of Adult Education in the United States*, Washington, D.C., 1960, pp. 41–53.

[3]Ibid., p. 51.

In summary, is it the purpose of continuing education to provide content, to pass on the culture, or is it the purpose of continuing education to help individuals and communities to develop, with emphasis on the learning process?

MOVING FORWARD VERSUS PREVENTING MOVEMENT BACKWARD

Today there is a good deal of emphasis in continuing education programs on what are commonly called coping skills. Individuals, often those who are deemed to be disadvantaged in some way, are helped to cope with their everyday lives. At another level, the same assumptions apply to many professional development programs. An engineer, nurse, or business executive needs help in keeping up with all of the changes that are going on in his or her profession, in the world of business, in society generally. Unless these professionals participate in continuing education, they will, in effect, slip backward. Most writers argue that people either move forward or slip backward; there is no standing still in a society that is constantly changing.

Is it enough for continuing education to be concerned with helping prevent people from slipping backward? Or is it the purpose of continuing education to help people move beyond coping to achieving some sense of control in their lives? This is, of course, a much more radical idea than coping, for to help people move forward, to help them take some control over their lives, may be upsetting to those individuals and institutions that control society.

Let's look at an example. Is it the purpose of continuing education to help low-income homemakers learn new recipes for preparing inexpensive foods and to learn new approaches to budgeting their limited incomes? Or is it a purpose of continuing education to help low-income homemakers organize a buyers' cooperative so they can purchase food at lower prices, to help low-income homemakers improve their job skills so they can earn more income, to help low-income homemakers who cannot work learn political skills directed toward more equitable welfare payments?

In the first instance, continuing education is helping prevent people from moving backward; it is helping them develop individual coping skills. In the second instance, continuing education is helping people move forward and together gain some control over their lives.

The Individual versus Society

Related to the issue of coping is another issue that continues to divide the field of continuing education—that of individual versus societal focus. Is it the purpose of continuing education to serve the individual or to serve society? One dimension of this larger issue revolves around the question of social change. Is it the purpose of continuing education to help people participate actively in social change, or is it the purpose of continuing education to help people adjust to and cope with social change?

Earlier, we referred to two different ways of viewing society—society as a collection of individuals, the sum of the persons who constitute it, versus society as an entity that is more than and different from the sum of the individuals that make it up.

But once we have assumed that society (community) is a distinct being, this does not necessarily imply that continuing education has any responsibility toward that society (community) and its needs and problems. In fact, some writers have emphatically argued against allowing continuing education to become involved with societal concerns—i.e., social change.

R. W. K. Patterson, a British philosopher, argues that when continuing education activities follow social change as an aim, two consequences will likely result: (1) continuing education will be turned into a political arena where social, economic, and political questions will become more important than educational questions, or (2) continuing education will become a political "closed shop," advocating a particular political approach.

Patterson argues that the appropriate aim of continuing education is to transmit knowledge which is "educationally worthwhile." Patterson defines education as "the fearless transmission of truth . . . [which is] . . . morally, socially, and politically neutral."[4]

Another British writer, K. H. Lawson, argues that continuing education is not synonymous with social service, recreation, or community work and cannot be justified in those terms. The only way that continuing education can be supported is for it to clearly show that it is a system of teaching and learning. Lawson sees teaching and learning in terms of an instructor providing inputs of ideas and information to learners.[5]

For most American writers, continuing education's involvement in social change is not an issue. Most, in fact, do not view social change as an alternative but rather emphasize continuing education's purpose as helping fill the needs of individuals. Some add that society can best be improved by educating individuals.

Werdell, for example, believes that if we concentrate our efforts on upgrading the educational level of individuals, the society, in turn, will be

[4]R. W. K. Patterson, "Social Change as Education Aim," *Adult Education* (English), vol. 45, pp. 353–359, 1973.

[5]K. H. Lawson, "The Concept of Purpose," *Adult Education* (English), vol. 43, pp. 165–170, 1970.

improved. He claims that "It is only through self-renewal of the individual that the society itself can be renewed."[6]

The upgrading of individuals has been emphasized by many continuing education programs such as those concerned with adult basic education, those that teach coping skills, and those that emphasize studying the great literature of the world.

Other writers concentrate solely on the development of individuals as the correct purpose for continuing education, without regard to the impact of individual development on society. For instance, Blakely writes, "I accept as the purpose of education the fostering of the growth of what is individual in each human being and the harmonizing of individuality with social unity, which unity should be based on a respect for individuality."[7]

Knowles and Klevins say, "The basic goal is to help individuals function more effectively in society and within their own community."[8]

In both the Blakely and the Knowles-Klevins definitions, the emphasis is on the individual and the individual "adjusting" or responding to society. The idea of social change, for the individual to work collectively with others to effect social changes, is not mentioned as a possible aim of continuing education.

A Canadian writes about the aims of continuing education in this way:

All sorts of definitions have been devised for "continuing education." They range through preparation for service to the State, promotion of virtue, gaining dominance over things, obtaining satisfaction of wants, and developing social efficiency. These things may be incidental, but isn't the real purpose of continuing education self-realization?[9]

We don't mean to overlook those who have promoted the idea that continuing education does have a role in social change. For example, Lindeman, back in 1926, wrote:

Adult education will become an agency of progress if its short-time goal of self-improvement can be made compatible with a long-time, experimental but resolute policy of changing the social order. Changing

---

[6]Philip Werdell, "Futurism and the Reform of Higher Education," in Alvin Toffler (ed.), *Learning for Tomorrow*, Random House, New York, 1974, p. 297.

[7]Robert J. Blakely, "What is Adult Education? Nine Working Definitions," *Adult Education*, vol. 5, pp. 131–145, Spring 1955.

[8]Malcolm Knowles and Chester Klevins, "History and Philosophy of Continuing Education," in Chester Klevins (ed.), *Materials and Methods in Continuing Education*, Klevins Publications, Los Angeles, 1976, p. 15.

[9]The Royal Bank of Canada, "Beauties of Learning," *The Royal Bank of Canada Monthly Letter*, Montreal, Canada, vol. 58, no. 11, p. 1, 1952.

*individuals in continuous adjustment to changing social functions—this
is the bilateral though unified purpose of adult learning.*[10]

Paul Sheats is another writer who advocates a social change function for
continuing education. But he cautions that continuing education should not be
considered to be synonymous with community action. In his view, "action
without planned, organized, purposeful citizen learning is likely to be unin-
formed, and certainly in some instances damaging to the common good."[11]

He makes an important point. Some people working in the field of
continuing education see all social action as continuing education. To be sure,
as we mentioned earlier, there is much to be learned from involvement in social
action activities. The point is, how much of this learning is random, and how
much is planned? The random learning will inevitably occur. Only insofar as the
learning is planned, organized, and purposeful, according to our previous
definition, can social action be construed as education.

Per G. Stensland makes a similar point. "Obviously all adult action is not
adult education. We are here concerned with that learning which includes study
and deliberation before and evaluation after the doing."[12]

This leads us to Paulo Freire's concept of praxis, the view that learning and
education take place only through the constant interplay of reflection and
action. For example, a group discusses and reflects on its situation and then
acts to change the situation. Again, the group reflects on its action and the new
situation created by its action before it acts once more. Reflection by itself,
unrelated to action, runs the risk of becoming what Freire calls verbalism—talk
without action. And likewise, action without reflection is not education either but
leads to mere activism or misguided activity.[13]

Though many American writers seem to emphasize the individual aspects
of continuing education, aiming to meet the needs of individuals, a few
American and some foreign writers emphasize the need for social action. For
example, Ravitz says, "If there is an immediate role for continuing education it
is to help us understand the urgency of our condition and the necessity to
refashion our societal institutions, including our economy. . . ."[14]

As we reflect on the discussion, the issue remains: Is it the purpose of

[10]Eduard C. Lindeman, *The Meaning of Adult Education*, Harvest House, Montreal, 1961
(First published in 1926).

[11]Paul Sheats, "What is Adult Education? Nine Working Definitions," *Adult Education*,
vol. 5, pp. 131–145, Spring 1955.

[12]Per G. Stensland, "What is Adult Education? Nine Working Definitions," *Adult
Education*, vol. 5, pp. 131–145, Spring 1955.

[13]Paulo Freire, *Pedagogy of the Oppressed*, Herder and Herder, New York, 1971.

[14]Mel Ravitz, "Sociological Implications for Adult Education in the Future," *Adult
Leadership*, vol. 25, no. 3, pp. 66–68, 1976.

continuing education to be concerned with the individual or with society? Should the field focus its attention on helping individuals grow, develop, and achieve self-actualization? Or should the field focus its attention on society and social change? Is it possible to focus on individual concerns and societal concerns both at the same time?

Vocational versus Liberal

In many ways this issue has captured more attention than the individual-society issue discussed above. This is particularly true at this writing, when fairly large numbers of people in this country are either unemployed or underemployed and when increasing numbers are seeking career changes.

Should not continuing education place considerable emphasis on vocational education programs, both those designed to prepare people for jobs and those designed to help people upgrade their jobs?

On the other hand, there are increasing numbers of people who are concerned with the quality-of-life issue, and they ask why continuing education is not more concerned with the quality of life or liberal education programs.

The issue is not a new one. Back in 1926, Lindeman separated vocational education from continuing education. He viewed vocational education as preparation for work but not as continuing education. "In the modern world of specialism only a small sector of personality is set into motion through vocational activities. We all tend to become specialists—which means that we all tend to become fractional personalities."[15]

In effect, Lindeman was saying that if we concentrate all our efforts on vocational education, we will not provide a total education. In fact, the person who pursues only vocational education will not achieve the kind of education that is important for his or her total life.

He goes on to say:

Adults who make bold to revive the once vivid interests of their total personalities will need to submit themselves to a process of reeducation. Their habit-systems will resist; the vocational organization in which they labor will continue its demand for specialized, partial functions; they will need to be motivated by ends which are either exterior or in opposition to the incentives which lead to pecuniary success. The whole of these environmental resistances tends to tempt the organism toward conformity; why go through the bothersome toil of reeducating my habits if the present ones serve to keep me alive, well-fed, well-clothed and well-housed?[16]

[15]Lindeman, op. cit., p. 34.
[16]Ibid., p. 35.

There are those who argue that our entire education system, from early childhood throughout the life spectrum, is focused on preparation for and carrying out of work—and for a particular kind of work, that of employment in large business and industry. For example, Oliver points out that the public schools prepare students for life as specialists in our modern industrialized society in often subtle ways.

By requiring teachers to draw up lesson plans and indicate behavioral objectives, both teachers and students become aware that they are accountable to the larger society in specific terms. Through the organization of schools in a fashion not dissimilar to corporate organizations, with managers at the top who are advised by technical specialists, the students are able to become accustomed to corporate organizations.[17] The school is seen as a production unit, with inputs and outputs and cost-benefit analyses.

Because our educational systems, at whatever level we wish to describe them, seem to reflect the prevailing values, attitudes, and directions of society, we learn something about the vocational-liberal split by looking at contemporary society itself.

Allport, for example, points out that apparently the sole objective of our society today is profitable, expanding production.[18]

Another and related dimension of contemporary society is technology. According to Webster Cotton, "Most social analysts would agree that science and technology have been the predominating influence in sharpening modern attitudes, values, and institutions."[19]

The connection between the corporation and technology is pointed to by Erich Fromm. For example, he sees our present society is being influenced by two guiding principles:

> . . . something ought to be done because it is technically possible to do it. If it is possible to build nuclear weapons, they must be built even if they might destroy us all. . . . Once the principle is accepted that something ought to be done because it is technically possible to do it, all other values are dethroned, and technological development becomes the foundation of ethics. . . . The second principle is that of maximal efficiency and output. . . . In order to reach this result, men must be de-individualized and taught to find their identity in the corporation rather than in themselves.[20]

[17]Donald W. Oliver, *Education and Community*, McCutchan Publishing, Berkeley, Calif., 1976, p. 20.

[18]Gordon W. Allport, "Values and Our Youth," in *Foundations of American Education: Readings*, Allyn and Bacon, Boston, 1969.

[19]Webster E. Cotton, *On Behalf of Adult Education*, Center for the Study of Liberal Education for Adults, Boston, 1968, p. 18.

[20]Erich Fromm, *The Revolution of Hope*, Bantam, New York, 1968, pp. 33–34.

Fromm goes on to say:

Man, as a cog in the production machine becomes a thing, and ceases to be human. He spends his time doing things in which he is not interested, with people in whom he is not interested, producing things in which he is not interested; and when he is not producing, he is consuming.[21]

If educational systems serve and reflect the societies of which they are a part, then we should not be surprised that educational systems would see as a major purpose a focus on preparing people for jobs, especially in a time of economic crisis. We would also expect that people would be prepared in a particular kind of way, i.e., to be efficient, to value science and technology above all, to be concerned largely with profit making, and to learn how to consume.

As we look at what is happening with educational systems operating today, we find much of what we would expect to find. A ringing cry of the early 70s which continues to the time of this writing is "career education." The U.S. Office of Education has promoted the concept for people of all ages. Those who promote the concept argue that the term should not be viewed as synonymous with "occupation" or "job." Instead the term should be viewed as a broad one which focuses on everything that contributes to helping people realize a sense of purpose and commitment to useful work.

Unfortunately, however, many educators tend to define career education as that education which will prepare people to fill one of the job slots listed in the job classification manual published by the U.S. Department of Labor.

What is happening in contemporary society is reflected in higher education as well. Donald K. Smith, senior vice president for academic affairs for the University of Wisconsin System observes:

A commonplace observation about higher education in the 1970's is that students are moving in large numbers from a stated preference for higher education aimed at personal development and a deeper under-standing of the civilization or culture of which they are a part toward preference for education with a stated occupational or professional goal. In the last decade, this has meant a reduction of approximately 20 percent, nationally, in the proportion of students seeking the baccalaure-ate degree in the liberal arts, and a corresponding increase in the

---

[21]Ibid., p. 40.

proportion seeking an occupationally or professionally oriented under-
graduate education.[22]

Smith does point out that in most professional and job-related educational programs some attention is paid to the liberal arts. Much popular writing, however, in both newspapers and magazines, emphasizes the economic dimensions of education, whatever the source, to the point where many people now view education as having an economic goal for them. What kind of job will I be able to get when I finish this course of study? How will participating in this workshop help me improve my job skills? This heavy emphasis on job preparation leads people who participate in such educational events as poetry writing workshops, music appreciation seminars, and history lectures to ask: In what way do you suppose this educational activity will help me in my job or help me get a better job?

In some ways it is understandable why educational agencies and institutions have and are putting so much emphasis on jobs and professions. It is a fact that large numbers of people are without work and even larger numbers are underemployed. It is a fact that many people are changing jobs, often because their old jobs were eliminated or provided inadequate salaries for changing needs. It is a fact that our society does stress production and consumption, with accompanying demands for competition and efficiency. It is a fact that education has demonstrated it can help prepare people for jobs, help them prepare for new jobs, and increase their competence in jobs they already have. But what are the consequences of this emphasis on vocational education?

Down through the years there has always been a healthy tension between liberal education and vocational education. Today, however, much liberal education is seen as frivolous and without purpose. Elementary schools in some states are cutting out music, art, and drama programs as unnecessary and not contributing to the "basics" that youngsters need for success in our society. The healthy tension between liberal and vocational education is disappearing. The emphasis has swung almost totally in the direction of vocational education. That shift has implications for those in the continuing education field.

SUMMARY

Over the years, much has been written about the purposes of continuing education. Often the literature poses apparently opposite purposes. In this

---

[22]Donald K. Smith, *Wisconsin Ideas*, University of Wisconsin System, Madison, Wis., vol. 1, no. 1, May 1976.

chapter we have explored four of these seemingly opposite positions about purpose: the developmentalist versus the rationalist approach, coping versus taking control, the individual versus society, and vocational versus liberal purposes. In the next chapter we will explore a rationale for deciding what the purposes of continuing education should be.

SUGGESTED READINGS

Cremin, Lawrence A.: *Traditions of American Education*, Basic Books, New York, 1977.

Faure, Edgar, et al.: *Learning to Be*, UNESCO, Paris, 1972.

Gardner, John W.: *No Easy Victories*, Harper & Row, New York, 1968.

Houle, Cyril O.: *The Design of Education*, Jossey-Bass, San Francisco, 1972.

Hutchins, Robert M.: *The Learning Society*, New American Library, New York, 1968.

Jensen, Gale, A. A. Liveright, and Wilbur Hallenbeck (eds.): *Adult Education: Outlines of an Emerging Field of University Study*, Adult Education Association of the USA, Washington, D.C., 1964.

————, ————, and————: *Perspectives of Adult Education in the United States and a Projection for the Future*, Department of Health, Education, and Welfare, Office of Education, Washington, D.C.

Verner, Coolie, and Alan Booth: *Adult Education*, Center for Applied Research in Education, Washington, D.C., 1964.

Whipple, James B., et al.: *Liberal Education Reconsidered*, Publications in Continuing Education, Syracuse, N.Y., 1969.

CHAPTER 7

A Rationale for Purposes

As the preceding chapter shows, those working in the field of continuing education disagree about what the purposes of the field should be. As we pointed out, often the purposes are dichotomized—some believe in the transfer of past and new knowledge while others stress development of people and communities; some advocate education for individuals where others suggest a social focus; some promote education with a primary vocational intent while others promote a more "liberal" education.

This diversity has tended to split the field. It has also confused those working in it, those preparing to work in it, and those responsible for making decisions that affect it—lawmakers, for example.

Given all this disagreement, how do we sort out what the purposes of continuing education should be?

Let's begin by reflecting back to our discussion of the nature of human beings. I assume that the purpose of continuing education is ultimately to serve people, their institutions, and their communities. It only follows, then, that any discussion of what the more specific purposes of continuing education should be ought to be grounded in our understanding of the human adult.

In Chapter 3 we took the humanistic view of human nature. We pointed out that human beings have characteristics in common with other animals—their need for water, food, shelter, and reproduction, for example. We saw that a person's life is determined both by internal factors, as the Freudians assert, and by environmental factors, as the behaviorists argue. We noted also that the life-span development research offers some clues as to what we might expect to happen in various stages of life.

But beyond all that, human beings also differ from animals. In fact, it is the dimension of human life which is not determined that clearly makes us human.

Here, for example, we refer to such characteristics as individuality, freedom, and the capacity for self-awareness. This means that we have the potential for self-direction even while part of our behavior is influenced by the environment and part by the unconscious.

Human beings also have a sense of the past, present, and future. They can think abstractly and with symbols. They can see themselves as others see them. They can empathize with others. They have the power to choose, although their choices are often accompanied by guilt, anguish, despair, and anxiety. Human characteristics include love, humor, guilt, shame, self-sacrifice, and appreciation of beauty.

Human beings have a basically social nature which enables them to work with others on a variety of social projects and to live in close relationship with their fellows.

Finally, human beings have the freedom to be active, not merely passive. In referring to what human beings are, we must always keep in mind what they may be in the future.

Unfortunately, many people are never given a chance either to discover or to express those aspects of themselves that are most human. Others apparently *choose* to suppress their own most truly human qualities or *submit* to repression, so that they indeed behave as Freud and the behaviorists suggest that they will. And, as we have pointed out above, educational systems have too often contributed to this process.

In a 1919 report of the Adult Education Committee of the British Ministry of Reconstruction, this problem and its consequences were underlined:

> *Too great an emphasis has been laid on material considerations and too little regard paid to other aspects of life. Getting and spending we lay waste our powers. Technical efficiency is but one element in national well-being. Our powers ought to be directed into wider channels in order that the intellectual and spiritual treasures of the race should be the heritage of all rather than the possession of a few, and so that the social virtues and the social spirit shall enjoy freedom of growth.*[1]

With this as background, let's move on to the purposes of continuing

[1] R. D. Waller (ed.), *A Design for Democracy*, Association Press, New York, 1956, p. 148.

education. Back in 1973, I explored this question and suggested the following as possible answers:

1. To help people make psychological adjustments to their social conditions and natural world by equipping them with the necessary knowledge, understanding, skills, and attitudes
2. To equip adults with the skills necessary for identifying and solving problems they may face, with an emphasis on the skills in solving problems and not on the content or subject matter
3. To help people change their social conditions
4. To help people become free, autonomous individuals[2]

At the end of my discussion about purposes in that 1973 publication, I wrote the following:

> *There are many questions that can be asked about overall purposes for adult education. A basic one is, should adult educators seek overall purposes for the field? Is the field so broad that overall purposes are not only impossible to determine, but may stifle the activities of individual adult education efforts? Should the overall purpose of adult education thus be to encourage multiple purposes? If, however, you believe there should be overall purposes, what is your stand on the four purposes listed above? Do you believe they should all be emphasized, or only one or two of them? Should all of these purposes be emphasized, but some emphasized more than others?[3]*

Now, five years later, I wish to expand that original list of suggested purposes. The purposes suggested below are all built on the assumption that the human being has both animal characteristics and uniquely human characteristics and that we must consider the totality of what constitutes human life.

In the broadest sense, then, the *purpose of continuing education is to enhance the quality of human life* in all its personal and social dimensions. More specifically, we suggest the purposes of continuing education should be the following:

1. TO HELP PEOPLE ACQUIRE THE TOOLS FOR PHYSICAL, PSYCHOLOGICAL, AND SOCIAL SURVIVAL

Within this purpose we can identify several subpurposes.

[2]Jerold W. Apps, *Toward a Working Philosophy of Adult Education*, Syracuse University Publications in Continuing Education, Syracuse, N.Y., 1973, pp. 37–38.

[3]Ibid., p. 38.

Work Skills

In our society, to provide for their food, clothing, and shelter, people must be gainfully employed. At least for the foreseeable future, work will take up considerable time for many adults. And justifiably, continuing education should be concerned about the preparation for work, assisting people who wish to acquire or improve their job skills and aiding those who wish to make career changes. Bailey suggests two essential purposes of education in relation to work:

> (a) to educate people to see their lives as a whole, that is to see the world of jobs in relationship to all other aspects of their waking hours, and (b) to educate those who are in a position to affect or exercise leadership . . . to engineer or catalyze experiments in personalizing and deroutinizing the world of work.[4]

Coping Skills for Day-to-Day Living

Our present society requires fairly sophisticated coping skills. We must know how to balance checkbooks, how to use credit cards, how to fill out job applications and tax forms, how to purchase intelligently, and how to live within the hundreds of laws that affect our daily living.

We must understand the health service agencies that are available to us. We should be aware of ways to prevent health emergencies through our knowledge of good nutrition, understanding of health maintenance, and involvement in exercise programs.

A legitimate purpose for continuing education programs is to help people gain these kinds of coping skills.

Skills for Interpersonal Relationships

Because human beings are social creatures they spend great amounts of time in the company of their fellows—in their homes, at work, and during leisure time. Yet skills for dealing with marriage tensions, children, neighbors, and people with whom or for whom we work are often poorly developed. This, too, should be an important area of concern for continuing education.

Skills for Leisure Time

In today's society, many people have increasing amounts of free time. Nearly everyone has vacation time, many workers have several three-day holidays

[4]Stephen K. Bailey, *The Purposes of Education*, Phi Delta Kappa, Bloomington, Ind., 1976, pp. 54–55.

during the year, some employers have cut work weeks to less than 40 hours. Our society has moved toward providing people with increasing amounts of leisure time—time away from work responsibilities—yet it has done very little in helping people learn how to use that leisure time. Boredom has become a disease for many people who detest their jobs and don't know how to use leisure time. The passive observer syndrome has overtaken many people. With each event, each TV show, each sports spectacular they observe, they look for more, something more daring, something more exciting, to break the grasp of boredom. Little is done to help people see alternatives to this constant pattern of passive entertainment.

Skills for Preserving the Natural Environment

Not until recently have people even become aware that they have problems in preserving the natural environment. Many believe that science and technology will ultimately pull us through and that we really don't have to worry about such matters as energy sources and pollution. Yet it has become abundantly clear that our relationship to our environment is critical and that it is in trouble. Our very survival on this planet requires that we develop skills for preserving the natural world.

Skills for Social Change

If our society is to survive, we must acquire skills for social change. Involved are such skills as understanding and being able to work with community power structures, dealing with conflict, participating in community problem-solving activities, determining future directions for a community, and organizing groups of citizens into pressure groups—to mention but a few of such skills. Underlying this purpose is the assumption that citizens have both the right and the responsibility to participate in social action. With careful involvement and use of knowledge, people can make appropriate decisions concerning the direction their society (or their communities) should take. Inherent in this purpose is the belief that citizens should not allow "experts" and specialists to decide concerning the future of their communities for them. Also inherent is the assumption that society can be deliberately changed through planning and the collective involvement of citizens. Too many citizens hold the belief that social change occurs indirectly and in spite of their activity. These people believe it is their task to learn how to adjust to the changes that are occurring.

The position taken here is that the survival of society requires active, organized involvement on the part of citizens in determining new direction for society. Continuing education can play a considerable role in helping citizens acquire the skills for such social change.

Skills for Problem Solving

Though in some ways implicit in all the skills mentioned above, skills in problem solving can make a great contribution toward helping people achieve physical, psychological, and social survival. Problem-solving skills are obviously necessary in social change, in coping with everyday living, in resolving interpersonal relationships, in dealing with leisure time, and in preserving the natural environment. In fact, in a wide variety of areas, skills in solving or in transcending problems will be highly useful (see Chapter 2).

Problem solving is best learned in the context in which problems exist. For example, one learns best how to solve community problems by participating in community problem solving.

We separate problem-solving skills from our list not because we mean to suggest that a separate and distinct effort should be made to teach problem solving but in order to emphasize that problem solving is a part of many educational situations. And, unfortunately, educators are often so intent on teaching facts and information that they don't take time to help people make use of the facts and information to deal with actual problems. It is as people learn how to work through their problems that the most lasting learning is achieved. Once a person has discovered a process for dealing with problems, then he or she can be much more self-directed in facing future problems.

2. TO HELP PEOPLE DISCOVER A SENSE OF MEANING IN THEIR LIVES

Beyond wanting to know what is necessary for them to survive, people also want to understand what human life is all about. They want to discover meaning in their lives. The search for and discovery of meaning in each person's life is what clearly sets us apart from other animals and all other life. It is one of the characteristics that makes our existence uniquely human.

An extremely important purpose of continuing education is to help people in their search for meaning, to help them achieve a sense of what is uniquely human in their lives. More specifically, continuing education can (a) help people discover and achieve personal creativity, (b) help people appreciate the satisfaction that goes with excellence, (c) help people benefit from emotional and intellectual discovery, and (d) help people discover their place in the world. These four examples are discussed below.

Helping People Discover and Achieve Personal Creativity

Here we have in mind the recognition, appreciation, and creation of beauty in all its varied forms. This may include appreciating works of art, literature, music, live theater, or dance. We are referring also to the thrill of canoeing on a quiet river at dawn, hiking to the top of a mountain on a summer day, and admiring wildflowers in a quiet meadow.

We also wish to include participation in various creative activities such as wood carving, creative writing, painting, acting, making music, or the host of other creative ventures through which we experimentally discover our talents and interests.

Bailey argues that,

> *How to offer instruction in the discipline and the emotional conditions conducive to personal enrichment through the arts is, or should be, a matter of highest educational priority. Whatever sense of national community is promoted by network sports and newscasts, we are being all but deadened aesthetically by the violence and inanities of most TV programming. Too often, education in the arts is considered a frill that can be discarded when budgets are tight. The shortsightedness of this value decision is appalling.[5]*

Helping People Appreciate the Satisfaction That Goes with Excellence

In many ways people in our society apparently have lost the sense of satisfaction that goes with doing a task well. Where emphasis these days is on "efficiency"—that is, completing a task in record time with minimum cost—excellence is often lost along the way.

We can discover something about ourselves and about what life means to us when we discover our talents and work toward achieving our fullest potential. But this means always striving toward higher levels of excellence in what we do.

When we don't have the opportunity to push toward developing our potential in our work, we may find a way to do so in our leisure-time pursuits. It is possible to find a sense of accomplishment and achievement in many of the avocational creative activities mentioned above.

In 1932, Everett Dean Martin warned what would happen to society if we continued to minimize the importance of achieving excellence. He wrote:

> *In the Eighteenth Century people were greatly concerned over the question of the fall of empires, and they formulated many theories to account for the decline and fall of the civilizations of the past. It seems to me that many of these theories were unnecessarily roundabout and labored, for I think it could be proved that every civilization that failed and passed away fell at the hands of barbarians.*

[5]Ibid., p. 67.

The barbarians of the past were savage creatures who lived somewhere outside the confines of the civilizations that they menaced. The barbarians of today are the barbarians in our midst. They dress like the rest of us. They wear trousers and wrist watches. They often operate machines. Sometimes they deliver lectures and preach sermons and edit papers. They may be clever, but their cleverness ends with their own utilitarian philosophy; it does not extend to the recognition of principles; it does not open the way for the insight that would bring mental freedom and mental maturity. Since we who are interested in education must be on guard against these barbarians in the modern world, it is well for us to be able to recognize their distinctive traits.

The first one is that barbarians, whether they live within or without, come in hordes. They look alike, they paint their faces alike, they use the same slang, indulge in the same passing fad, repeat the same standardized, newspaper-editorial-derived opinions, read the same tabloids, crave the same sensations, look at the same motion pictures, listen to the same radio programs.

Barbarians like big things. They do not discriminate. They want violent sensations. . . .

Barbarians tend to destroy what they cannot understand. Anything that they cannot understand is wrong. Hence, the destruction of Rome, the resistance to the Renaissance. The barbarian mind is controlled by custom and taboo and herd opinion; it discourages intellectual variation and novelty.

Finally, barbarians are adolescent, almost infantile in their point of view. Their world is a world of magic. They believe that the universe is governed by principles that correspond to their own infantile wishes: they wish a thing to be so, it must be so. Education is powerless to reach people who cannot see beyond the projection of their own desires. The only education that can prevent the development of this stultifying point of view is adult education, mature education. Training people merely to respond to the stimuli of fact, drilling them in habits, whether they be habits of thought or action, cannot do it. Mature education initiates people into the world of principles; it frees their minds.

What we need is enlightenment, and we need a great deal of it, and we need it badly. No civilization can exist in which men fail to achieve excellence of some kind.[6]

[6]Everett Dean Martin, "Wanted: Enlightenment," *Journal of Adult Education*, June 1932, pp. 293–294.

Helping People Benefit from Emotional and Intellectual Discovery

Too often in our society we emphasize the pragmatic worth of an activity or thing. We ask, what will we gain by doing this? How will doing this allow us to make more money or help us solve some problem we have?

By emphasizing the practical we lose the excitement and the value of doing something for the sake of doing it. We could use many examples. Our interest may be wildflowers. We may work at identifying all the wildflower species in a park near our home. It may take us years to accomplish this task, considerable digging in reference books, perhaps even a course in biology or ecology. And for what purpose? The purpose is the sense of meaning and satisfaction one gets from the discovery of a previously unidentified wildflower species. The purpose is the thrill of searching through the flower guidebooks, attempting to identify a new species. The ends and means are the same. The doing, the search, is the goal of our wildflower identification exercise. The process has no economic value; no social problem will be solved by it.

Reading is one of the most usual approaches toward emotional and intellectual discovery. "Great reading . . . is a search for wisdom through interaction with ideas compellingly expressed on the printed page. . . . It creates explosions of insights and sunbursts of aesthetic pleasure."[7]

Helping People Discover Their Place in the World

There is probably nothing so alienating as not knowing where one fits in the order of things. Questions like "Who am I?" and "What is the meaning of my life?" often begin with an understanding of relationships. How do I relate to those around me—my family, my peers, those with whom I work, those who live in my community? How do I relate to myself? How do I relate to my historical and cultural roots? How do I relate to the natural world? How do I relate to time and to space?

Obviously we cannot begin to answer these age-old questions in the following few paragraphs. But we do want to emphasize the importance of raising the questions and to suggest that continuing education should accept the responsibility for helping people wrestle with these questions.

The basic problem of relationships raises many questions. "How do I relate to those people around me" can often be translated into the need to feel needed, the need to feel useful to others.

"How do I relate to time" involves a search for relationship to the past and the future. At this writing, a great many people are making an avocation of

[7]Bailey, op. cit., pp. 72–73.

searching for their own historical roots. They are deriving great satisfaction from this, as well as a sense of identity.

But there is also a great deal of cynicism in our society. People reflect on the past only long enough to see what has been bad about it, dismiss their history, and claim they wish to "live in the here and now." Obviously, while one lives in the here and now one is also influenced by the past and hope for the future. We must remember that those who forget the past are condemned to repeat it.

In our materialistic striving for more money and possessions, we sometimes forget about the human being's unique place in the universe.

> *The insistent message of the prophetic geniuses of history is that there is a qualitative difference between man and beast—that man has the capacity to enter a special relationship with the universe and that this special relationship is man's glory and meaning. . . . We despair because we have forgotten our place in the universe, because we have become so preoccupied with man as animal and man as object that we have forgotten man as creative spirit and man as noble subject.*[8]

And, on the other hand, we try to forget sometimes that we have characteristics in common with all living matter and that we too are a part of the natural world. As such, we are influenced by the coming and going of the seasons, by the birth and growth and death that is the cycle of life on this planet.

It is in delving into questions such as these that people begin to discover some aspects of who they are and what life means to them. It is in delving into such questions that people begin to explore what makes them human, what makes them an integral part of the order of things but at the same time sets them uniquely apart.

3. TO HELP PEOPLE LEARN HOW TO LEARN

Too often, we in continuing education forget the obvious. We forget that one important task we have is to help people learn how to learn, so that they can sever their dependence on teaching institutions. In this country, people have traditionally been taught without being given much, if any, responsibility for organizing what they plan to learn.

This attitude has understandably carried over into the minds of adults. If they have never experienced any other approach to education than having

[8]Ibid., p. 74.

someone else organize and present information to them, this is what they will expect.

Gross claims that

Because our thinking about learning has been dominated for so long by the image of the school, we know virtually nothing about the potentialities for truly individual learning, or about how the other institutions of a society can become adjuncts to and resources for the learning process. . . . We do not know, in short, how to seize back for the individual the power over the growth of the mind, or what to do with the power once we gain it.[9]

But if adults are to become autonomous learners who can achieve control of their own learning, they then will need to learn how to learn. We in continuing education can play an important role in the process.

4. TO HELP COMMUNITIES (SOCIETY) PROVIDE A MORE HUMANE SOCIAL, PSYCHOLOGICAL, AND PHYSICAL ENVIRONMENT FOR THEIR MEMBERS

The three previous purposes have focused on the individual. Now we turn our attention to the community or the society in which individuals live. We take the position here that one does not change society only by focusing attention on the individuals that make up that society. True, some changes can be made in society following that approach. But often some of the more dramatic and important changes that are necessary in a society are not made by focusing on individuals but on the institutions that compose a society and the relationships of these institutions to the people. Continuing education, too, must address itself to institutions and social organization as well as to individual learning.

Often, no matter how many skills, no matter how much knowledge, no matter how much attitudinal change is achieved in individuals, the society will not be changed. Why? Because the society simply won't let it happen—or, to be more precise, because some groups perceive that their interests will be adversely affected if society changes in certain directions. Roadblocks are created, as it were, to prevent people who have the new knowledge and skills from effecting the changes.

Saul Alinsky became acquainted with this problem in the course of his work on the streets of several large United States cities. He learned that the society,

---

[9]Ronald Gross, "After Deschooling, Free Learning," in Ivan Illich et al. (eds.), *After Deschooling What?* Perennial Library, Harper & Row, New York, 1973, pp. 158–159.

as represented through its power structures, must be dealt with directly. He began to teach people that society is changed by challenging it and organizing large groups of people for change, not by providing education to isolated individuals.[10]

Miles Horton recognized the problem in his work in union organizing and later in the civil rights movement and with the poor in Appalachia. He brought local citizens to Highlander, his residential center, where they learned about themselves and their communities. Most important, they learned skills they could use in working with their communities to change them.[11]

And Paulo Freire experienced at first hand the problem of community change in Brazil, where he developed an approach to adult literacy, working especially with peasants. This approach utilized discussion groups in which the participants were enabled to confront the system that oppressed them.[12]

Thus, we conclude, an important purpose of continuing education is to help communities (society) become aware of the type of psychological, social, and physical environment they are providing for their members. Once the awareness has been effected, continuing education should include the purpose of helping communities to correct, or at least respond to, those problems that are discovered, those shortcomings that prevent human beings from living humane lives. These processes are variously called "community problem solving," "community development," and "community improvement." The label doesn't matter, but the effort does. Continuing education cannot be effective if it chooses to focus all its efforts on helping individuals. Some important emphasis must be placed on attempting to help the communities themselves.

The Need for Balance

As mentioned at the beginning of this section on purposes, the overarching aim of continuing education should be to improve the quality of human life. To do that, we cannot emphasize one set of purposes over another; we cannot say that vocational education is more important than education in the arts nor can we say the opposite. Human beings must be treated holistically. There must be an attempt to integrate thinking with feeling, the personal with the social.

It is easy for us in education to focus on pieces, to emphasize, as many people do today, the idea that education for work should take precedence over other kinds of education. But in doing so we are not considering the totality of

[10]For a description of the approaches that he advocated, see Saul Alinsky, *Rules for Radicals: A Practical Primer for Realistic Radicals*, Random House, New York, 1971.

[11]Frank Adams, *Unearthing Seeds of Fire*, Blair, Winston–Salem, N.C., 1975.

[12]Paulo Freire, *Pedagogy of the Oppressed*, Herder and Herder, New York, 1971.

human existence. It is as true today as in biblical times that "Man does not live by bread alone."

Thus we cannot be content simply to accept the dichotomies outlined in Chapter 6. We must attempt to transcend the apparent either/or nature of this problem of purpose and hold together both poles of the dichotomy at the same time. That is, we must attempt to provide content and also teach process; we must help some people move forward while at the same time helping to keep others from slipping backward; we must pay attention to the individual but at the same time not lose sight of society; we must focus on vocational concerns and at the same time be concerned about liberal education. We must, as Krishnamurti writes, help people "see the significance of life as a whole. . . . the purpose of education is not to produce mere scholars, technicians and job hunters, but integrated men and women who are free of fear."[13]

SUMMARY

We have argued in this chapter that continuing education should be guided by the overall goal of improving the quality of human life. Four subpurposes were suggested: (1) to help people acquire the tools for physical, psychological, and social survival; (2) to help people discover a sense of meaning in their lives; (3) to help people learn how to learn; and (4) to help communities (society) provide a more humane social, psychological, and physical environment for their members.

Finally, we said that continuing education must seek to achieve balance as it strives to attain its purposes, for human beings must be seen as wholes.

SUGGESTED READINGS

Apps, Jerold W.: "Accent on Social Philosophy: Some Questions for Adult Educators," *Adult Leadership*, February 1972, p. 280.

Bradford, Leland P.: "Toward a Philosophy of Adult Education," *Adult Education*, vol. 7, no. 2, pp. 83–93, Winter 1957.

Broudy, Harry S.: "The Philosophical Foundations of Educational Objectives," *Educational Theory*, vol. 20, no. 1, pp. 3–21, Winter 1970.

Carnegie Commission on Higher Education: *Toward a Learning Society*, McGraw-Hill, New York, 1973.

Cotton, Webster E.: *On Behalf of Adult Education*, Center for the Study of Liberal Education for Adults, Boston, 1968.

[13]J. Krishnamurti, *Education and the Significance of Life*, Harper & Row, New York, 1953, pp. 14–15.

Cremin, Lawrence A.: *Traditions of American Education*, Basic Books, New York, 1977.

Edel, Abraham: "What Should Be the Aims and Content of a Philosophy of Education," *Harvard Educational Review*, vol. 26, no. 2, pp. 119–126, Spring 1956.

Faure, Edgar, et al.: *Learning to Be*, UNESCO, Paris, 1972.

Hiemstra, Roger: *Lifelong Learning*, Professional Educators Publications, Lincoln, Neb., 1976.

Hallenbeck, Wilbur C.: "Building Working Philosophies in Adult Education," *Adult Education*, vol. 3, no. 5, pp. 148–152, May 1953.

Hutchins, Robert M.: *The Learning Society*, New American Library, New York, 1968.

Illich, Ivan: *Deschooling Society*, Harper & Row, New York, 1970.

Lengrand, Paul: *An Introduction to Lifelong Education*, Croom Helm, Ltd., London, 1970.

Mead, Margaret: "A Redefinition of Education," *NEA Journal*, vol. 48, pp. 15–17, October 1959.

Meiriam, Sharon: "Philosophical Perspectives on Adult Education: A Critical Review of the Literature," *Adult Education*, vol. 27, no. 4, pp. 195–208, 1977.

Reich, Charles A.: *The Greening of America*, Random House, New York, 1970.

Roszak, Theodore: *Where the Wasteland Ends*, Doubleday, New York, 1972.

SECTION IV

CONTENT FOR CONTINUING EDUCATION

The questions of what should be taught (the content for continuing education), and how this content should be organized (curriculum development) have faced educators of all times and places. These questions are particularly troublesome for the field of continuing education.

Some professionals in continuing education have attempted to adapt curriculum development approaches designed originally for elementary education. Others have taken essentially noneducational models, such as social action theory, from sociology and attempted to apply them to continuing education contexts. Still others program "ad hoc"; that is, they take an informal, pragmatic approach that essentially has no conceptual base.

In the three chapters comprised by this section, we will examine the questions of what content is and how it should be organized. In Chapter 8, we discuss several viewpoints on knowledge. In Chapter 9, we look at some of the problems associated with the Tyler approach, the Freire approach, and the liberal education approach. Then, in Chapter 10, we offer some guidelines for the development of new approaches to curriculum development in continuing education.

CHAPTER 8

Viewpoints on Knowledge

What should be taught is a question educators have faced for as long as there have been educators. Thus it is not unusual for those in continuing education to ask the same question. Now, however, the context of the question is the education of adults. What should adults be taught?

In this chapter we will explore the problems associated with what should be taught. More specifically, we will examine the concept of knowledge and the various viewpoints that educators have about knowledge.

THE NATURE OF KNOWLEDGE

Many people define knowledge simply as the sum of what is known—facts, concepts, principles, theories. Others would say that knowledge is made up of the conclusions reached by such traditional disciplines as physics, mathematics, psychology, history, philosophy, and sociology.

Still others, both within and outside the field of continuing education, attack these definitions of knowledge as being too narrow. They would ask: What of a person who is skilled at playing tennis—is this knowledge? What of experiences one may have, such as feeling the satisfaction of performing a difficult feat, the thrill of observing a full moon in autumn, or the pleasure of intimacy with another person—are these feelings a kind of knowledge? And what of a newly discovered process for doing something, an approach or method that is new—does this constitute knowledge?

Quickly we discover that the question of what knowledge is is not easily answered. The answers we do find often disagree with each other; indeed, they sometimes seem contradictory or even unrelated.

If we are to understand curriculum, we ought to explore these various positions on the nature of knowledge and then attempt to make some sense of what we have discovered.

Absolute versus Changeable

Let's begin by looking at knowledge as an absolute versus knowledge that is subject to change. Absolute knowledge is not subject to change. It is eternal and is passed on through the generations.

Two criteria for absolute knowledge are that (1) it must be certain and not open to doubt and (2) it must not be inferred. By "not inferred" is meant that it must not be based on some prior knowledge claim. The following are some examples of absolute knowledge: the whole is larger than its parts; there is a past, a present, and a future; and human beings occupy space in the universe.

"A knowledge claim that is certain and uninferred (not dependent upon a prior knowledge claim) can be used as a spring-board from which to deduce or discover other knowledge that is not self-evidently true, as are the certain and uninferred truths."[1]

Those who subscribe to the position of absolute knowledge agree that although the amount of absolute knowledge is small, that which is known is sure and certain, providing a stable base on which to build further knowledge.

Those philosophers who subscribe to the position that knowledge is subject to change argue that there can be knowledge which is not based on certain and uninferred premises. While these people admit that such knowledge may not be 100 percent reliable,

> [they are] content with this type of probabilistic knowledge for [they are] convinced that we deal always with possibilities and probabilities and never with certainties . . . [Their] response, therefore, is that philosophy must emulate science in posture and learn to be content with knowledge that is open to change, rather than final; relative, rather than absolute; probable rather than certain.[2]

These philosophers believe that nothing can be verified beyond any

[1]Charles J. Brauner and Robert W. Burns, *Problems in Education and Philosophy*, Prentice-Hall, Englewood Cliffs, N.J., 1965, p. 12.

[2]Ibid., p. 13.

possibility of doubt, yet they are content with the knowledge they have. When new evidence becomes available that refutes some existing knowledge, they freely replace the old with the new.

When we compare these two approaches to knowledge, we find those who believe in the absolute approach arguing that information gained through scientific means is something less than true knowledge. "Knowledge worthy of the name is absolute, it is certain, and since these terms can never be applied to the results of empirical inquiry true knowledge is metaphysical and not empirical—and it is this kind of true knowledge that should be possessed. . . ."[3]

Knowledge based upon human experience, that gained through empirical means,

> while useful, is of less ultimate value than knowledge of metaphysical realities—as, for example, in philosophy or theology—which is gained only by a mind trained to recognize self-evident truths and, by application of proper logic, to reason out even more subtle truths. . . . The well-stocked mind, then, does contain some empirical information of use (it could not be otherwise), but the truly well-stocked mind also possesses a good quantity of higher quality information—absolute, certain, metaphysical knowledge.[4]

On the other hand, those who promote the view of knowledge as subject to change criticize the absolutists both in terms of the means they suggest for the development of knowledge (logical reasoning based on self-evident truths) and the ends of the process (possession of knowledge for its own sake).

Frederick C. Neff, in a criticism of the absolute approach to knowledge, writes:

> Needless to say, such a system resulted more in continually reaffirming conventional creeds than in anything like fresh or vital modes of inquiry. In fact, honest inquiry was virtually impossible, for such a system required that the premises of logic consist of a proposition already firmly established by traditional outlooks. Since no new conclusions could emerge, intellectual disciplines consisted largely in mastering the rules of logic, rather than in questioning or inquiring. As Francis Bacon has stated it, "The present system of logic rather assists in confirming and rendering inveterate the errors founded on vulgar notions, than in searching after truths; and is therefore more hurtful than useful."[5]

[3]Ibid., p. 39.

[4]Ibid.

[5]Frederick C. Neff, "Six Theories of Intellectual Discipline," *Educational Theory*, vol. 7, no. 3, p. 164, July 1957.

Realism, Idealism, Experimentalism

Another way of looking at the nature of knowledge is to analyze it from the perspectives of realism, idealism, and experimentalism.

Realism presupposes that the categories by which we apprehend the external world have a reality of their own. That is, they exist in the external world and not just in our minds.

"The universe is made up of real, substantial entities, existing in themselves and ordered to one another by extra mental relations. These entities and relations really exist whether they are known or not."[6]

Idealism presupposes that universals are in the structure of the mind, not in the external world. Knowledge is then the discovery of these structures of the mind, or "ideas."

The idealist perspective is one of an interdependence between the knower and the known. "Knowledge is possible, but it is knowledge of things whose existence is dependent on the knowledge process. . . . In all forms of Idealism, great stress is placed on mind or intelligence in knowledge. . . ."[7]

According to Edward A. Krug, idealists center their attention on the human mind in the creation and perception of knowledge. Knowledge, in their view, includes human insights, appreciations, appraisals, and decisions—a rather broad definition.

"Idealism is frequently associated with the concept of liberal education, that is the kind which is aimed at human freedom, particularly intellectual freedom; the liberal subjects are deemed most likely to provide for the cultivation of the free intellect of personality."[8]

Experimentalists see knowledge as being based upon ever-changing experience; it cannot be separated from action. John Dewey, an advocate of this definition of knowledge, puts heavy emphasis on the process of problem solving and the interrelationship of ends and means. That is, the ends of education become the means to further education—the process cannot be separated from the product. The discussion of knowledge cannot be separated from the context in which the person is dealing with a problem.

Dewey claims:

The method of intelligence manifested in the experimental method demands keeping track of ideas, activities, and observed consequences. This is a matter of reflective review and summarizing, in which

[6]John Wild, "Education and Human Society: A Realistic View," *Modern Philosophies and Education*, Fifty-Fourth Yearbook of the National Society for the Study of Education, Part I, The National Society for the Study of Education, Chicago, 1955, p. 17.

[7]Edward A. Krug, *Curriculum Planning*, Harper & Row, New York, 1957, p. 71.

[8]Ibid., p. 74.

there is both discrimination and record of the significant features of a developing experience. To reflect is to look back over what has been done so as to extract the net meanings which are the capital stock for intelligent dealings with further experiences. It is the heart of intellectual organization and of the disciplined mind.[9]

For Dewey then, knowledge is equated with experience, but experience that is thoughtfully considered.

This approach to knowledge is shared by Paulo Freire, who writes about the need for praxis—the interrelation of action with reflection. For Freire, too, knowledge is the result of people's interaction with their world and their attempts to transform it. Knowledge cannot be separated from the context of the situation or the people who are dealing with that situation.[10]

As Krug summarizes:

Knowledge from [the perspective of experimentalism] is an aspect of ever-changing experience and is inseparable from action. Experimental processes furnish the knowledge needed for solving particular problems . . . experimentalists emphasize the development of the creative and intellectual powers of the human individual plus the fostering within every individual of a sense of social responsibility and concern for others. Intellectual powers, however, are looked upon in terms of reflective thinking skills as applied to the solution of individual and social problems.[11]

Theoretical, Empirical–Statistical, Personal–Social

According to Severyn T. Bruyn, knowledge has three forms: theoretical, empirical–statistical, and personal–social.[12] Theoretical knowledge includes systems of relationships among facts.

Theory is a system for handling data (facts) in such a way as to provide a framework for describing and explaining a situation. The functions of theory are: "(1) to enable prediction and explanation . . . ; (2) to be useful in theoretical advance [of a discipline or field of study]; (3) to be usable in practical

[9]John Dewey, *Experience and Education*, Macmillan, New York, 1938, p. 109.

[10]Paulo Freire, *Pedagogy of the Oppressed*, Herder and Herder, New York, 1971.

[11]Krug, op. cit., pp. 72–75.

[12]Severyn T. Bruyn, *The Human Perspective in Sociology*, Prentice-Hall, Englewood Cliffs, N.J., 1966, pp. 172–173.

applications—prediction and explanation should be able to give the practitioner understanding and some control of situations; (4) to provide a perspective . . . a stance to be taken toward data; and (5) to guide and provide a style for research. . . ."[13]

Empirical–statistical knowledge includes organized categories of facts that are determined by some empirical process such as survey, experimentation, or structured interview. In addition, this type of knowledge is presented in numerical form, which provides the opportunity for statistical treatment.

Personal knowledge can be referred to as privately held knowledge.

The number of people who may hold this "private knowledge," however, is relative to the case in point. Many people have a personal knowledge of baseball in the United States. The term personal directs attention to that which is experienced by the individual, although the basic elements of that knowledge can be shared by others. People in a large nation can develop a personal knowledge of that nation that is widely shared because of mass communication systems; the members of a sizable ethnic group can have a personal knowledge of suffering from discrimination which they feel collectively and personally. The term personal simply emphasizes that the experience is an individual one.[14]

Social knowledge "may include personal elements in it (e.g., individually felt attitudes and sentiments), but it emphasizes an interactive awareness of shared expectation in a human group. It is a consciousness of the positions and roles taken by people in the organization of a group."[15]

Bruyn argues from the perspective of one doing research about human beings and emphasizes that all three forms of knowledge—the theoretical, the empirical–statistical, and the personal–social—are necessary before one can *know* about a human situation or answer a human-related research question.

Classical versus Romantic

Robert M. Pirsig talks about the division of human understanding into classical and romantic.

A classical understanding sees the world primarily as underlying form

[13]Barney G. Glaser and Anselm L. Strauss, *The Discovery of Grounded Theory*, Aldine, Chicago, 1967, p. 3.

[14]Bruyn, op. cit., p. 173.

[15]Ibid.

itself. . . . [It] proceeds by reason and by laws—which are themselves underlying forms of thought and behavior. . . . [It] is straightforward, unadorned, unemotional, economical and carefully proportioned. Its purpose is not to inspire emotionally, but to bring order out of chaos and make the unknown known. It is not an esthetically free and natural style. It is esthetically restrained. Everything is under control.[16]

On the other hand, romantic understanding is described in terms of an immediate appearance. "The romantic mode is primarily inspiration, imaginative, creative, intuitive. Feelings rather than facts predominate. 'Art' when it is opposed to 'science' is often romantic. It does not proceed by reason or by laws. It proceeds by feeling, intuition, and esthetic conscience."[17]

These two forms of knowledge, classic and romantic, are vastly different from one another. If we were to take Pirsig's approach one step further, we could divide classic knowledge into empirical and rational knowledge. Empirical knowledge, as suggested above, is obtained through some kind of measuring, some kind of observation by a human being of a situation or phenomenon. Rational knowledge, on the other hand, is derived from first principles through a process of deductive thought. Scientific knowledge is derived from a combination of two approaches to knowing, the use of senses and reason. Thus scientific knowledge is a combination of empirical knowledge and rational knowledge.

But, as Pirsig argues, scientific knowledge is not the totality of knowledge. There is another broad area that he refers to as romantic knowledge which is perhaps especially associated with the arts.

Many people tend to identify with one or the other type of knowledge— scientific or romantic. Seldom do these two approaches to knowledge seem to come together.

The problem of the rift between scientific knowledge and romantic knowledge will be discussed in greater depth in Chapters 13 and 14, where we explore research approaches in continuing education.

Manipulation of Symbols
Related to the idealist perspective is the approach to knowledge used by mathematicians and logicians. These people determine knowledge by the elaboration and manipulation of the symbols of their fields. By following long-standing mathematical procedures, mathematicians are able to derive

[16]Robert M. Pirsig, *Zen and the Art of Motorcycle Maintenance*, Morrow, New York, 1974, pp. 73–74.

[17]Ibid., p. 73.

knowledge. By following accepted approaches to logical thought, logicians likewise derive knowledge.

Fact, Feeling, Skill

Still another way to look at knowledge is to think about it in terms of knowledge that deals with facts, knowledge that includes feelings, and knowledge that is skill-related.

Most descriptions of knowledge, as we have outlined above, tend to deal with knowledge in some factual sense. However, knowledge also includes the feelings or emotions that people experience. Feelings are an important part of the human experience; people love and hate, feel joy and depression. Why not consider our consciousness of these emotions as knowledge?

Likewise, what of skills? One can read several books about swimming and yet not be able to swim a stroke. And, of course, one can be an excellent swimmer and yet *know* very little about the facts of swimming.

It would seem appropriate to consider skills, then, as another form of knowledge, a *how-to* form of knowledge as contrasted with *what, why, when,* and *where* kinds of knowledge.

SUMMARY

The concept of knowledge is not as simple as it may appear to be. We have looked at knowledge from several viewpoints: (1) knowledge which is absolute versus that which is subject to change; (2) knowledge from the perspectives of realism, idealism, and experimentalism; (3) knowledge from a theoretical, empirical–statistical, and personal–social perspective; (4) classical versus romantic knowledge; (5) knowledge as symbol manipulation; and (6) knowledge from the perspectives of fact, feeling, and skill. How we conceptualize knowledge not only affects our understanding of the process of knowing—the teaching–learning process that we will discuss later—but also what we mean by the process of curriculum development in continuing education. This leads us to the next chapter.

CHAPTER 9

Problems with Planning Approaches

If we would agree that curriculum for continuing education consists of knowledge, we now have some idea of the breadth for such a curriculum, given the various types of knowledge described in Chapter 8. In this chapter we will explore the problems associated with three approaches to curriculum development for continuing education: (1) the Tyler approach, (2) Freire's approach, and (3) the approach of liberal education.

But before we begin, let us recognize the problem of terms concerning curriculum in the field of continuing education.

PROBLEMS WITH TERMS

In traditional schooling, the term "curriculum" is used. The dictionary defines it as a set of courses offered by an educational institution. This is a rather commonly accepted definition. But for many people in continuing education, the term "curriculum" is too narrow. Educators of adults like to think of what is taught in continuing education as broader than a set of courses.

Thus many people in continuing education use the term "program" to denote that which is taught. Of course, there are many problems with this term too. The word "program," to many people, means an event or an activity such as a musical program or a radio program, both of which may or may not have an educational intent. Or people think of a program as a printed outline of what is to follow. One of the dictionary's definitions for "program" is "a plan or system under which action may be taken toward a goal." That is quite close to the meaning that many educators would agree on.

In our discussion here, we will be using both the words "curriculum" and "program" to mean what is taught in continuing education.

This leads us to the question of how the curriculum or program in continuing education is determined. With a few notable exceptions, most of the curriculum development models in continuing education literature are based on the work Ralph Tyler did back in the late forties and fifties.

THE TYLER APPROACH

Ralph W. Tyler, in his now famous *Syllabus for Education 305*, asked four questions: "(1) What educational purposes should the school seek to attain? (2) What educational experiences can be provided that are likely to attain these purposes? (3) How can these educational experiences be effectively organized? (4) How can we determine whether these purposes are being attained?"[1]

Modifications of Tyler in Continuing Education

Some writers in continuing education simply changed a word here and there and adopted the Tyler approach in its entirety. For example, Lynn Pesson, in an essay on extension program planning, suggested that the following questions should be asked when an educational program within the cooperative extension service is being planned:

> *What educational purposes should the Extension Service seek to attain? What educational experiences can the Extension Service provide that are likely to attain these purposes? How can these educational experiences be effectively organized by Extension personnel? How can Extension personnel determine whether these purposes are being attained?*[2]

The Tyler approach, based on the four basic questions, usually includes the following steps. Occasionally different terms are used; but with some careful

[1]Ralph W. Tyler, *Basic Principles of Curriculum and Instruction*, The University of Chicago Press, Chicago, 1950, pp. 1–2.

[2]Lynn L. Pesson, "Extension Program Planning with Participation of Clientele," in H. C. Sanders (ed.), *The Cooperative Extension Service*, Prentice-Hall, Englewood Cliffs, N.J., 1966, p. 94.

examination, the reader will find the Tyler model explicit in most of the approaches. (We cite several below.) These steps are:

1. Identify needs.
2. Define objectives, preferably in behavioral terms.
3. Identify learning experiences that will meet these objectives.
4. Organize the learning experiences into a plan that has scope and sequence.
5. Evaluate the outcomes of the effort in light of the objectives established in step 2.

Cyril O. Houle describes the following "Decision points and components of an adult educational framework":

1. A possible educational activity is identified.
2. A decision is made to proceed.
3. Objectives are identified and refined.
4. A suitable format is designed.
5. The format is fitted into larger patterns of life.
6. The plan is put into effect.
7. The results are measured and appraised.[3]

Though Houle mentions seven "decision points and components," they bear a close resemblance to Tyler's five steps.

Malcolm Knowles devotes separate chapters in his book *The Modern Practice of Adult Education* to each of the following topics: (1) assessing needs and interests in program planning, (2) defining purposes and objectives, (3) designing a comprehensive program, (4) operating a comprehensive program, and (5) evaluating a comprehensive program.[4] The chapter headings are remarkably similar to Tyler's listing.

Patrick Boyle says the program development (curriculum development) process includes the following phases:

(1) Analyze the social system (society, community) and clientele. Collect and analyze situational data, facts, and trends to effectively understand the situation. . . . (2) Identify desired outcomes. . . . (3) Design instructional plan. . . . (4) Program of action. Select the content, activities and events which should . . . create awareness and interest . . . provide the

[3]Cyril O. Houle, *The Design of Education*, Jossey-Bass, San Francisco, 1974, p. 47.

[4]Malcolm S. Knowles, *The Modern Practice of Adult Education: Andragogy versus Pedagogy*, Association Press, New York, 1970.

learning experiences necessary to help learners attain the expected outcomes. . . . (5) Accountability of resources. Plan evaluation into each of the programming phases.[5]

Tyler's Assumptions

Tyler does not explicitly state his assumptions about such matters as human needs, educational objectives, and the nature of knowledge. But the following assumptions are implicit in his approach:

1. An educational program should be based on the needs of learners. Tyler, and those in continuing education who have adapted his approach, has raised the emphasis on learner needs to slogan proportions. Almost all the literature on continuing education includes a statement such as the following: "Continuing education programs are based on the needs of people."

2. It is possible, empirically, to determine the needs of learners and thus have a basis for writing educational objectives. The three sources of objectives are studies of learners, studies of contemporary life, and suggestions from subject-matter specialists. According to Tyler, one decides on the needs of learners (as expressed in educational objectives) by combining information from all three sources and then filtering this information through philosophical and psychological screens.

3. Knowledge is external to the learner; it is "out there" for the learner to obtain. This assumption comes from Tyler's suggestion that subject-matter specialists should be consulted about what knowledge they believe the learners should have—what knowledge the learners need.

4. Objectives are the basis for organizing learning experiences. Although Tyler has modified his position somewhat on behavioral objectives,[6,7] he still advocates their use in organizing an educational program.

5. Curriculum development is a stepwise process. One begins with the identification of needs and ends with some kind of evaluation effort. Tyler does say that an educator may at times find that the plan which has been developed needs to be modified.

[5]Patrick G. Boyle, *Problem Solving Programming*, University of Wisconsin—Madison and Extension, Madison, Wis., 1977, pp. 10–14.

[6]G. L. Carter, Jr. (ed.), *Facilitating Learning with Adults: What Ralph Tyler Says*, Division of Program and Staff Development, University of Wisconsin— Extension, Madison, Wis., 1976.

[7]June Grant Shane and Harold G. Shane, "Ralph Tyler Discusses Behavioral Objectives," *Today's Education*, September–October 1973, pp. 41–46.

There was a time when people thought the world was largely static— when the long-term plan was a one-way road. You got started and you'd eventually come up to the end. But this is not the nature of planning that I think is important today for adult educators. Planning is a continuously tentative view of what to do next.[8]

6. The emphasis of educational effort is on the individual learner. Tyler does not discuss education for social change with an emphasis on changing society rather than changing the individual.

Comments on Tyler's Assumptions

Because the Tyler approach to planning is followed by so many people in continuing education, it is essential that we examine his assumptions with some care. Below we look at those assumptions relating to learner's needs, behavioral objectives, the stepwise approach to curriculum development, and survival-based learning.

Learners' Needs Implicit in Tyler's approach is the assumption that needs are important and, second, that it is possible to determine empirically what these needs are.

R. F. Dearden asks:

Is it simply a matter of carrying out the relevant piece of research to determine what [learners'] needs are, so that problems of curriculum and of learning, which have been somewhat intractable and centers of dispute in the past, can now be handed over to the sociologist or psychologist for definitive solution? In other words, are questions as to what people need purely empirical?[9]

Usually need is conceived in terms of something that is absent. A 45-year-old truck driver lacks a high school diploma, therefore he *needs* one. A welfare mother lacks knowledge and skill in balancing her low-income budget, therefore she *needs* these skills and knowledge. A pharmacist lacks sufficient continuing education units (CEUs) to maintain his license to practice, therefore he *needs* these CEUs so that he will be able to continue his practice.

But there is more to need than the idea that something is lacking or absent.

---

[8]Carter, op. cit., p. 27.

[9]R.F. Dearden, "Needs in Education," in Martin Levit (ed.), *Curriculum: Readings in Philosophy of Education*, University of Illinois Press, Urbana, Ill., 1971, p. 89.

The absence of a state of affairs does not create a need unless this absence ought not to exist, for example, because then a rule would not be complied with, or a standard would not be attained, or a goal would not be achieved. In short, "need" is a normative concept and, as such, needs are not to be determined just by research into what is observably the case.[10]

A commonly used definition of need is the gap created when we compare *what is* with *what should be.* This definition puts the question of how one determines needs directly into focus. We can determine what is through empirical means, but what should be is a normative question and cannot be determined solely by surveys, study of census materials, interviews, and the like.

The should-be question is probably the most difficult one in the entire curriculum-planning process. Who should determine it—the learners, the educators of adults, the power structure in the community, the elected decision makers (such as a city council, the county board, or the state legislature)? All these have been involved in determining should-be answers for adult learners. For example, state legislatures in some states have deemed it necessary that people in certain professional fields take part in specified amounts of formal continuing education every year. In this situation, need is easily determined simply by comparing the amount of continuing education the professional has had to date with the standard established by the state legislature.

Even if there is broad agreement that state legislatures can appropriately determine professional requirements for a great many areas, the should-be question is not answered, and thus the concept of need becomes a difficult one. What minimal standard of living should all Americans be able to expect? We have never been able to arrive at consensus of what the answer to that question is or how it should be answered. What minimal basic education does everyone need in our society? Again, there is considerable debate.

In many situations the should-be answer is assumed. In the example of the truck driver who does not have a high school diploma, the assumption is that everyone *should* have a high school diploma. But is that a reasonable assumption? Or would it be more reasonable to find out something about the kinds of problems the truck driver is having or the challenges he wishes to meet, so that continuing education along those lines might be provided?

The point is that the normative aspect of determining needs, the identification of what should be, cannot be accomplished by purely empirical means. It always requires judgments based upon commitments to certain values. But the extent to which a norm is being attained or the precise way in which it is not

[10]Ibid., p. 90.

being attained *can* be determined empirically. That is, if we have an identified goal or standard or have otherwise answered the should-be question, we can then determine through appropriate scientific means whether or not the should-be question is being answered or the specific manner in which it is not being answered.

"It can be seen that needs-statements do at least have an empirical basis. They can, accordingly, be empirically refuted, for example, by pointing out that the norm is in fact being attained . . . or by showing that what is said to be needed will not in fact do the trick and so cannot be what is really needed."[11]

But norms

. . . can neither be "discovered" nor empirically refuted, since they indicate how things ought to be in various ways. Questions as to desirable standards, proper functioning, desirable rules, or what appropriateness and efficiency are cannot be determined by observation or experiment, though this does not mean that they are arbitrary or insusceptible of being reasoned about. It does mean, however, that conflicts of opinion may be expected here, that in some cases the conflict may be very intractable and that . . . decisions may be involved, not just discoveries. . . . [12]

In a democratic society we are committed, at least in theory, to answering should-be questions through public discussion, argument, and debate by which we arrive at a working consensus.

Behavioral Objectives   As we mentioned above, since writing his syllabus in 1950, Tyler has somewhat modified his concept of behavioral objectives. Nevertheless, many adult educators continue to follow the syllabus. For this reason we need to examine the problem of behavioral objectives.

The reasons given for using educational objectives, whether they be written in behavioral terms or not, are essentially two: (1) they serve as a guide for organizing action and designing learning experiences and (2) they can serve as a basis for determining results of the learning activity, comparing what happened with what was planned.

An implicit assumption about objectives is that a planner of educational programs can decide *before* an activity, class, or workshop what the outcomes of that activity ought to be. Further, the assumption, insofar as knowledge is

---

[11]Ibid., p. 93.
[12]Ibid., p. 94.

concerned, is that knowledge tends to lie outside the person and that objectives are a systematic plan for bringing the learner and the knowledge together. Depending on our assumptions about the nature of knowledge, we will either accept or reject this dimension of objectives.

What are the problems when we use behavioral objectives in designing educational programs? We could raise several questions: Is everything that is learned demonstrable behaviorally? For example, if we have gained some new insight into our life from reading a novel, can this learning be demonstrated behaviorally? (Here, I reject the idea, for example, that a person who has written an essay entitled "Three Insights I've Gotten from Reading a Novel" has given adequate evidence of a change in behavior.)

Is it ethically appropriate for an educator, or anyone else for that matter, to determine what behavior another human being should display? Does this not involve the risk of enabling educators to manipulate the learning process as they happen to see fit?

There are other practical reasons why behavioral objectives pose problems. One stems from the fact that it is impossible for the educational planner to anticipate all the learning that will come out of a particular learning experience.

Some educators have prepared long, tortuous lists of behavioral objectives, sometimes referred to as competencies, to the point of absurdity. And still, in any learning experience, unanticipated learning will occur. The question is, should this unanticipated learning be discarded in any evaluation, should attention be paid only to the previously determined behavioral objectives? How do we evaluate these different learnings?

Still another problem with previously determined behavioral objectives has to do with flexibility.

Once a learning activity begins, it may become obvious that the focus of the activity should be changed and the objectives modified. Indeed, the students may demand that a change be made. This may mean abandoning some previously determined objectives, modifying others, or adding new ones. If the teacher has to adhere to a pre-planned set of behavioral objectives, these options are impossible.[13]

All this is not to suggest an abandonment of planning for learning and the abolishment of educational objectives in continuing education programming. Our discussion here is focused on previously determined, often inflexible *behavioral* objectives.

[13]Jerold W. Apps, *Toward a Working Philosophy of Adult Education*, Publications in Continuing Education, Syracuse University, Syracuse, N.Y., 1973.

Stepwise Approach to Curriculum Development An assumption of Tyler's approach, and of every approach patterned after it, is that curriculum is planned in a "first you do this and then you do that" style. This is a reductionist assumption. That is, it is assumed that the whole equals the sum of its parts, and that it is possible to take apart the curriculum development process and deal with each of the pieces one at a time, in sequential order.

As we shall see in the next section, when we discuss Freire, this assumption doesn't always hold. In fact, it is often impossible to consider a series of steps in a sequential order.

For example, Tyler argues that we must first search for needs, then write objectives, then plan learning experiences, and finally evaluate the process to see whether we have accomplished anything.

But can we not imagine a different approach to learning? For example, a group of farmers gathers to talk about a superhighway that will cut through their farms. Nothing has been planned ahead of time. No educational objectives have been established nor learning experiences planned other than a group discussion. And from the first meeting the group members decide on next steps, what information seems necessary, and what means would be appropriate for obtaining that information. How should they organize their responses to the highway plan—should they oppose its construction, suggest an alternate route for the highway, or should they attempt to reorganize their farming operations to cope with the new highway and the new arrangement of space?

Likewise, would it not be possible for a group of adults interested in studying Wisconsin history to meet together and discuss the topic, deciding what they want to do next as they go along?

In other words, is it possible for an educator to look at an educational situation in its entirety without first dissecting it into little parts, often before the learner ever comes into the picture?

Survival-Based Learning If we believe that the overall purpose of continuing education is to help enhance the quality of life, then educational programming must go beyond helping people cope with the problems they face in day-to-day living—how to get and keep a job, how to get along with their spouses and their children, how to stay financially solvent, and all the rest of the skills and knowledge we need to survive in our society.

Much of the Tyler approach, particularly as it has been adapted by various educators of adults, focuses on survival skills. When we ask the question "What are the problems the adults in our community face?" we are asking about problems in survival. When we say we want to base our educational programs on the needs of the learners, what we are usually saying is that we want to base our educational programs on some area of concern which relates to survival. As we indicated in the chapter on purposes, continuing education has a considerable responsibility for helping people survive in our society. But there is much more to human life than survival.

In my judgment, most of those educators who use or adapt the Tyler approach stop short of providing opportunities for people to go beyond survival, to grapple with what it means to be human, to discover hidden talents and potentials, to enlarge perspectives, to increase esthetic appreciation, or to improve and enhance their institutions and communities.

We turn now to an educational perspective with quite differing assumptions about education.

THE FREIRIAN APPROACH

The Freirian approach to continuing education is relatively new. People in North America did not know about Paulo Freire and his work in South America to any great extent until the translation and publication of his book *Pedagogy of the Oppressed* in 1971. Since then there has been considerable discussion of his approach and some small number of attempts to apply his ideas in North America, Europe, and some Third World countries.

Freire stresses the importance of the social and political context in which education occurs. For Freire, an educational program consists of two phases: "(1) *thematic research* and (2) *the educational program*. The two together *both* constitute the overall educational program; research and future program curriculum, methodology or process and content are to be conceived as a unified whole."[14]

Thematic research is the process by which people begin to grasp their particular social reality, expressed as a series of interrelated themes or topics. "Thematic investigation will seek to identify significant themes, establish links between themes, and, in the process, pose these themes (with their implied opposites) as problems—all viewed within the historical-cultural context of the people."[15] Typical themes, for example, might include work, unemployment, and poverty.

Thematic research results from the interaction of educators and learners and is itself to be viewed "as education, cultural action, part of the liberation process—not merely as a preparation for education."[16]

[14]Arthur Seldon Lloyd, "Critical Consciousness and Adult Education: An Exploratory Study on Freire's Concept of Conscientization," unpublished M.S. thesis, University of Wisconsin—Madison, Madison, Wis., 1974, p. 60.

[15]Ibid., p. 61.

[16]Ibid., p. 64.

The educational program phase includes making presentations to people in "circles of culture," Freire's term for small groups of people (no larger than twenty). The themes drawn from the previous research are posed as questions or problems. In presenting these themes, the educators use visual materials such as slides and photos. They also use newspaper articles, stories, poems, dramatizations, and similar modes for suggesting themes. Within the culture circles, coordinators, who are preferably local persons trained in Freirian methods, lead the discussions.

Freire places heavy emphasis on the involvement of people in his educational approach. Four levels of involvement are evident in a Freirian program:

(a) the initial participation by volunteers from the selected population in the investigation and planning phase; (b) recruitment of local people, as far as possible, as coordinators; (c) the involvement of as many people as possible in a given community, area, region or even nation—but in small groups; and (d) within each culture circle, participation by all persons, avoiding domination of the discussions by either coordinators or by the local minority.[17]

Before saying more about the Freirian approach, let us examine some of the assumptions upon which the approach is based.

Freire's Assumptions

1. Education is never neutral. That is, education either helps people liberate themselves or it contributes to their loss of freedom and humanity. For Freire, there is no such thing as value-free education or education that is impartial.

2. Human beings are free to act on their world. They have the alternative of being able to create and modify their world and themselves, as compared to animals who lack this ability. People are able to reflect on their past, be conscious of the present, and make plans for the future. Nevertheless, we are historical and social beings. Our actions and reflections occur within specific social situations and, to an extent, are limited by these situations.

3. The focus of education includes changing the structure of society as well as the social situations in which people live. In this process, individuals themselves change—whether through learning to read and write or, more fundamentally, through changing their consciousness of themselves as per-

[17]Ibid., p. 73.

sons. In other words, Freire has organized an educational process in which the participants have changed from passive, isolated victims to active subjects capable of learning and acting together.

4. The approach to dealing with societal problems should be dialectical. Freire characterizes our time as one of domination and dependence: the domination of the many by the few; the dependence of the masses—"the oppressed"—on those who hold power—"the oppressors." The purpose of education is to help the oppressed liberate themselves from their oppressors. In this process, the oppressors, too, become liberated as they cease being oppressors.

5. The process of education is holistic. That is, one does not first do some type of survey to determine needs, then write learning objectives, then plan learning experiences, and so on. The Freire facilitator works from the beginning with a group of people and, through a dialogical process, seeks to raise the level of consciousness of a group concerning their social situation and themselves in relation to each other and this situation. Thus the Freire approach begins with the assumption that people may not always be able to verbalize their most fundamental problems—that only through a process of consciousness raising are these subsurface problems brought into the open and discussed. These, in turn, open up awareness of broader needs and problems. Freire refers to this process as "problem posing."

Freire also emphasizes praxis, the interrelationship of action and reflection. That is, during the process of consciousness raising, a group of persons, as they reflect on their problems, decides on a course of action in an attempt to respond to these problems. After trying some action, they once more come together to discuss (reflect on) their action before they attempt another action. (Dialogue itself is part of this action—and an especially significant action for those living in what Freire has called a "culture of silence.")

6. Knowledge occurs in the process basically through two reciprocally related activities. The coordinator (Freire's term for "educator") provides an analytical framework through which the participants' experience of their society is examined. Often, in the process of responding to problems, specific knowledge—research information, facts, ideas, opinions of outside resource people—is needed. In addition, the participants' own experience, brought to awareness through the reflection and problem-posing process, constitutes a major source of knowledge.

Freire is highly critical of education that conceives of knowledge as something to be distributed. He describes traditional education as "an act of depositing, in which the students are the depositories and the teacher is the depositor. Instead of communicating, the teacher issues communiques and makes deposits which the students patiently receive, memorize, and repeat. This is the 'banking' concept of education in which the scope of the action allowed to the students extends only as far as receiving, filing, and storing deposits."[18]

7. The educator who follows the Freire approach is a facilitator who guides but does not direct, who is more concerned to raise questions than to provide answers.

Examples of the Freirian Approach

Scattered around the world are a number of examples of the Freirian approach. Freire has written about his own experiences in literacy training in Brazil.[19]

Various other people have attempted to apply the Freirian approach in a variety of settings and for purposes other than literacy training.

James DeVries attempted to apply this approach to agricultural extension work in Tanzania.[20]

Chere S. Coggins describes several attempts to apply Freire's ideas in North America. She cites (1) a University of Wisconsin—Madison adult education seminar organized around the Freirian approach; (2) a group of workers in Santa Cruz, California, organized to look at community problems; (3) a meat-boycott awareness group in Madison, Wisconsin; and (4) a group of "social animators" in Montreal, Canada, who worked in a poverty-ridden area in that city.[21]

Comments on Freire

The Freirian approach is not without its critics. Because this approach, in many ways, represents quite a radical departure from the traditional ways of thinking about education, such criticism is to be expected.

Vagueness of Freire's Writing A criticism of many who read Freire's work is that it is difficult to understand. Bruce Boston, who bills himself as a loving

---

[18]Paulo Freire, *Pedagogy of the Oppressed*, Herder and Herder, New York, 1971, p. 58.

[19]See Paulo Freire, *Education for Critical Consciousness*, Seabury, New York, 1973, and "Cultural Action for Freedom," *Harvard Educational Review* and Center for the Study of Development and Social Change, Monograph Series No. 1, 1970.

[20]James DeVries, "Agricultural Extension and the Development of Ujamaa Villages in Tanzania: Toward a Dialogical Agricultural Extension Model," unpublished Ph.D. dissertation, University of Wisconsin—Madison, Madison, Wis., 1978.

[21]Chere Sandra Coggins, "Application of the Freire Method in North America: An Exploratory Study with Implications for Adult Education," unpublished M.S. thesis, University of Wisconsin—Madison, Madison, Wis., 1973, pp. 34–35.

critic of Freire, writes "it ill behooves an educator for liberation to present himself to interested readers cloaked in such an obscure, convoluted, dull, overly metaphysical style, devoid of the real human experience which generates provocative ideas. . . . even theory can be clearly written, and even more important humanly written."[22]

Of course, part of the problem with the writing is that it is not only a translation from the Portuguese—the translator may need to share some of the criticism—but the style of writing is also quite foreign to American readers. In defense of Freire, much of the criticism of his writing relates to the book *Pedagogy of the Oppressed*. This was actually his *second* book. He first wrote *Education as the Practice of Freedom*, which discusses his adult literacy programs. Unfortunately, *Pedagogy of the Oppressed* was translated into English and published in the United States three years before this first book (contained in *Education for Critical Consciousness*). It is somewhat easier to grasp Freire's ideas if one first reads *Education for Critical Consciousness*.

Emphasis on Political Revolution Some people who read Freire are disturbed by his emphasis on revolution. In describing the radical who subscribes to Freire's beliefs, Griffith writes:

> *Freire's ideal radical would not tolerate the views of those who were not ready to accept the conclusion that revolution is essential. It is at this point that Freire's pedagogy parts company with democratic ideas and all educational philosophies which seek to arrive at truth by permitting the free expression of error as a means of exposing its limitations.*[23]

On the other hand, Freire does advocate that discussion groups (circles of culture) operate completely on democratic principles.

Emphasis on Dialectical View Freire's view of the world is one of dualities. For example, a Freirian group working in California discovered the following themes in its work: husband versus wife, children versus parents, community

---

[22]Bruce O. Boston, "Paulo Freire: Notes of a Loving Critic," in Stanley M. Grabowski (ed.), *Paulo Freire: A Revolutionary Dilemma for the Adult Educator*, ERIC Clearinghouse on Adult Education, Syracuse, N.Y., 1972, p. 86.

[23]William S. Griffith, "Paulo Freire: Utopian Perspective on Literacy Education for Revolution," in Stanley M. Grabowski (ed.), *Paulo Freire: A Revolutionary Dilemma for the Adult Educator*, ERIC Clearinghouse on Adult Education, Syracuse, N.Y., 1972, p. 73.

versus no community, landlords versus renters, social change versus despair and escape (drugs), new customs versus old customs, jobs versus unemployment, students versus the school system, church versus the faithful, and culture group versus television.[24]

Critics of this approach say it leads to artificial polarization and actually creates conflict. Further, it is argued that this approach is far too simplistic, particularly for advanced societies that may involve an array of relationships, not only those who are for and those who are against something.[25]

Many argue that it is the purpose of education to attempt to build bridges between divergent points of view rather than to deliberately attempt to create more chasms. For some, the Freirian approach appears designed, at least initially, to create chasms. Others, however, would argue that the Freirian approach merely recognizes already existing conflict.

Lack of a Specific Process Many people, particularly action-oriented educators of adults, upon reading Freire's work make such comments as "But what are we supposed to do with this? Where do we start? How do we get organized? What is supposed to happen when? What roles and functions does the educator of adults have in all this? Where does the program planner fit into what Freire is saying?"

Freire has chosen deliberately not to offer a specific, carefully spelled out, stepwise method. His belief is that the application of his approach is situational—that is, what works in one situation may not work in another. He feels that it is the educator's responsibility to work out specific methods with the people in their given situation.

He has attempted to offer guidelines as to what educators might do. But for those educators who are accustomed to quite carefully laid out blueprints, Freire's guidelines are not enough.

A related criticism is the length of time required by the process. Particularly in North America, there is a stress on efficiency in education, but the process of consciousness raising is often quite time-consuming. Dialogue and the process of reflection-action-reflection takes time. Many educators of adults don't believe they can afford the time it takes to properly conduct a Freirian educational program.

Coordinators and People Another concern of those who consider the Freire approach is the relationship of the coordinator (adult educator) to the people

[24]Coggins, op. cit., p. 57.
[25]See Lloyd, op. cit., pp. 158–165, for a discussion of this issue.

(learners). What will prevent the coordinator, who has probably had more extensive training and experience than the people, from lecturing to the people rather than engaging in dialogue with them? In other words, what will prevent the coordinator from assuming the more traditional educational role of simply giving people information—what Freire calls "banking"? Will not the educator guide the direction and determine the outcome of the discussions? This is particularly a problem when the people expect the educator to assume a dominating role—a banking role.

Similarly, how will the coordinator prevent the development of a dependency relationship with the people? The coordinator is viewed as leader, and many people have accepted the premise that a leader should be a person with answers to the people's questions. If the leader does not have answers, then why is he or she the leader?

These problems inherent in the Freirian approach are serious. And some critics find no clear or satisfactory answers on how to deal with them in the literature.

THE APPROACH OF LIBERAL EDUCATION

The third approach to developing a curriculum for continuing education is in some ways more abstract than the Freirian approach. The literature of continuing education is scanty on approaches to curriculum development that emphasize liberal continuing education. In some ways, this approach is more a philosophy than it is a methodology, and it has been around for a long time, going back as far as the Greeks.

Within the recent history of continuing education in this country, an emphasis on liberal education for adults has tended to come and go. At this writing, liberal education is on a downswing.

Let's begin our discussion of liberal education and curriculum development by looking at some of the assumptions.

Assumptions of the Liberal Education Approach

1. The focus of liberal education is a concern for human beings in their humanity. Frank Rhodes, President of Cornell University, cites John Henry Cardinal Newman's ideas about a liberal education: "[Newman] confronts us today, provoking us to a more profound inquiry into the ultimate nature of our humanity, urging us to embrace knowledge, not as an abstraction to be savored in isolation, but as a guide to and a servant of a life of openness, of freedom and of high purpose. . . ."[26]

[26]Frank H. T. Rhodes, "A Continuing Vision of Truth, Faith and Knowledge," *The Chronicle of Higher Education*, Feb. 6, 1978, p. 40.

As Freda Goldman points out:

No matter what approach, content, method, or organization is used, the distinguishing feature of liberal education is its view of man as the central figure in a ground of things. When liberal educators are doing what they ought to be doing, they are worrying not so much about poverty as about poor people, not about perfecting systems but about producing people who can cope with systems, not about making a good society, but about developing good men. But the temptation is always in the other direction . . . we are ensnared into dealing with things instead of with man.[27]

2. Liberal education focuses on learning basic principles that transcend life's problems and situations. It is in this area that liberal education is most fundamentally different from that education which prepares people to work and survive in a scientific, technical, and industrial nation.

What are some of these basics?

[A liberal] education should give a person a clear conscious view of his own opinions and judgments, a truth in developing them, an eloquence in expressing them. It teaches him to see things as they are, to go right to the point, to disentangle the skein of thought, to detect what is sophistical, and to discard what is irrelevant. It prepares him to fill any post with credit and to master any subject with facility.[28]

Those who subscribe to the idea of liberal education find today's formal schooling inadequate to the extent that it focuses on functional knowledge and skills. This judgment also includes much of continuing education:

The system is open and go, and the knowledge and skill [one] acquires today is obsolete tomorrow. The essence of modern life is change, while modern man seeks stability. So liberal education must find a way to equip the individual with the competence and sense of competence to shape and cope with a world whose future is unknown. We are engaged in a twentieth-century renaissance in which there lives a twentieth-century renaissance man who is continuously being and becoming, making and shaping, and feeling comfortable with. uncertainty and

[27]Freda H. Goldman, "Foreword," in James B. Whipple, Kenneth Haygood, Freda H. Goldman, and Peter E. Siegle (eds.), *Liberal Education Reconsidered: Reflections on Continuing Education for Contemporary Man*, Publications Program in Continuing Education, Syracuse University, Syracuse, N.Y., 1969, pp. 1–2.

[28]Frank H. T. Rhodes quoting John Henry Cardinal Newman, op. cit.

ambiguity. In this renaissance thing-oriented education is an obsolete concept, for things learned today are inadequate for tomorrow. On the other hand, the personal attributes developed today form the basis for continuing learning throughout life.[29]

Mortimer Adler, one of the developers of the great books program, says:

. . . the Great Books deal with the basic problems, both theoretical and practical, of yesterday and today and tomorrow, the basic issues that always have and always will confront mankind. The ideas they contain are the ideas all of us have to think about. The Great Books represent the fund of human wisdom, at least so far as our culture is concerned, and it is this reservoir that we must draw upon to sustain our learning for a lifetime.[30]

Not all liberal educators would agree that the great books as defined by Adler are the only source of content for a liberal education, which leads us to the next assumption.

3. Liberal education balances process and content. The Center for the Study of Liberal Education for Adults defined its content around four broad areas: social and political issues, community participation, ethical and moral values, and the arts.[31]

The tendency, though, in much liberal education is to define the content around such traditional areas of study as the arts and sciences. That is, the curriculum is organized around specific, discrete courses such as English literature, art appreciation, music history, and philosophy of science.

But not only is the content of liberal education important—the process matters as well. In fact, to many liberal educators, the process is *as important* as the content.

One thing is essential to becoming human, and that is learning to use the mind. A human being acts in a human way if he thinks. . . . The education the world is seeking is one that helps everybody learn to think. Since everybody has a mind, there is at least a probability that he can

[29]Peter E. Siegle, "Einsteinian Man" in James B. Whipple, Kenneth Haygood, Freda H. Goldman, and Peter E. Siegle (eds.) *Liberal Education Reconsidered: Reflections on Continuing Education for Contemporary Man*, Publications in Continuing Education, Syracuse University, Syracuse, N.Y., 1969, pp. 99–100.

[30]Quoted in Malcolm S. Knowles, "Philosophical Issues that Confront Adult Educators," *Adult Education*, vol. 7, no. 4, p. 235, Summer 1957.

[31]Whipple, op. cit., p. 18.

learn to use it. . . . This, in turn, implies the capacity to distinguish the important from the unimportant. It implies the development of critical standards of thought and action.[32]

The Center for the Study of Liberal Education for Adults suggested that the "process" of a liberal education occurs in varying degrees within an individual. An individual:

(1) increases his interest in the particular situation; (2) increases his knowledge and his understanding of the relationships among the phenomena, hypotheses, and concepts of systems of ideas in the area; (3) and ultimately increases his skill in critical judgment, including the ability to examine and modify his value system to make it more coherent, more compatible with his knowledge and understandings.[33]

Given these assumptions about liberal education, what does the concept of *curriculum* mean? And how does an educator who is interested in liberal education go about planning a liberal education curriculum?

Liberal Education Curriculum Planning

There are no carefully worked out recipes for planning a liberal education curriculum. What often occurs is that an institution such as an extension program of a college or university will offer a series of courses, often noncredit, in the area of liberal education. For example, there may be courses on literature, courses on values and ethics, courses in art, and the like.

The process used in planning these courses is often informal. Someone is interested in teaching a course, say, on contemporary American fiction. The instructor organizes the course and orders the books, the course is promoted in the community, and if the minimum number of students enrolls, the course is taught. There are no elaborate needs-determination procedures. Nor is there a systematic attempt to involve the anticipated learners in the planning of the course, although some of this is often done informally so that the curriculum planner can get some feel for the potential students' interests. Plainly and simply, someone decides to teach something, it is promoted, and then it is taught.

Who decides what should be taught? This will vary. Often it is the teacher of a given liberal studies area. Sometimes an administrator of continuing

[32]Robert M. Hutchins, *The Learning Society*, Praeger, New York, 1968, pp. 90–91.
[33]Whipple, op. cit. p. 18.

education programs decides that a given area of study should be emphasized. Occasionally but quite rarely, citizens from the community may suggest a topic area to be considered.

An example of a liberal education program is the Rhinelander School of Arts sponsored by the University of Wisconsin–Extension each summer in northern Wisconsin. A small group of planners–administrators of community arts programs for the University of Wisconsin–Extension—do the bulk of the planning, organizing, and promoting of the program. This program consists of noncredit workshops (continuing education units are offered) in various phases of creative writing, including poetry, playwriting, nonfiction, and fiction as well as a program in children's dramatics and offerings in painting and drawing.

Because this particular liberal education program has been conducted in the Rhinelander community for many years, a small but important group of local citizens is consulted about the program direction. The local consultants for the program are the cultural leaders in the community rather than the rank-and-file citizen, the person who works in the paper mill, or the homemaker with five small children.

Another way programs in liberal education are planned is to put the planning responsibility on the shoulders of the person who is seeking an education. That is, a liberal education program can be an entirely self-directed program in which the student selects books to be read, plays to attend, or whatever he or she chooses.

Professionals in continuing education can assist this process by offering consultation or referral to people who are attempting to organize their own liberal education programs. Aware of liberal education opportunities that exist in the community, they can respond to a person's proposed education plan, making suggestions based on their work with others who have developed similar plans and based on their knowledge of what is available.

Thus, in this case, each liberal education program is uniquely tailored to fit the needs of the individual who is planning it.

Comments on the Liberal Education Approach

Those who develop curriculum around the ideas of liberal education are not without their critics. These critics say the following:

1. Liberal education is elitist. A liberal education is only for those who already have considerable education and want to continue their learning in areas with which they may already be familiar, such as literature or art. Also, those who enroll in liberal education programs are usually the middle-class professionals, those who both can afford the programs and have the time to participate. It is difficult to find any sizable cross section of "ordinary" citizens participating in liberal education programs, such as unemployed and poor people, minorities, working men and women, farmers, and the like.

Liberal education is also criticized as being elitist because the programs are planned with little or no involvement on the part of those who will participate in the programs. Someone other than the participant is making decisions about what a program should be. Of course, a major exception to this is the self-directed liberal education program that we discussed in the preceding section.

2.   Liberal education programs are not practical. This is one of the most cutting criticisms of liberal education curriculum efforts. People ask: How will this program help me get a job, a better job, or perhaps help me keep the job I now have? How will this kind of educational offering help me make more money? How will this kind of educational opportunity help me compete better in the business world?

On another level, people often say: How can a study of history or of literature make any difference in my life today? What difference does it make that something happened 2,000 or 10,000 or 10 years ago? What is important is what is happening today and what will happen tomorrow.

Liberal educators are usually able to respond to all these questions. But the fact remains that large numbers of college-trained young people in the liberal arts have had great difficulty finding employment. Given this reality, what motivation is there for an adult who needs job retraining to be interested in a liberal education program?

3.   Liberal education is too costly for its benefits. There are many people today who think in terms of cost-benefit. Given so many dollars of investment for an education, how many dollars of benefit—in increased employment, for example—can we expect in return?

The criticism is also offered in less economic terms. Critics of liberal education programs say: "Show us how people who are involved in liberal education programs have changed their behavior as the result of their involvement." Or, more gently, "Show us, in terms you'd like to choose, how people who are involved in liberal education programs have benefited from their involvement." Often, liberal education is hard-pressed to answer these questions.

As a result of this and the second criticism, many tax-supported liberal education programs for adults have been severely cut in recent years. Decision makers have decided that more practical, more economically efficient programs (those which a cost-benefit analysis formula will fit) should be given higher priority when funding decisions are made.

4.   Liberal education programs focus on the individual. Those who are interested in social change, who believe that social change is brought about by focusing on social structures and collective action rather than limiting attention to the individual, criticize liberal education for its individualistic orientation.

These critics argue that social change will never occur—i.e., social improvement is impossible—when all educational efforts are focused on the individual. The focus of educational effort must be on the society—the community—as a whole.

SUMMARY

We examined three approaches to continuing education curriculum planning: (1) the Tyler approach, (2) the Freirian approach, and (3) the approach of liberal education. For each approach, we examined the assumptions, gave a few examples of its application, and then presented some of the shortcomings of the approach. We are now ready to move to the next chapter, where we present guidelines for designing new approaches to curriculum development in continuing education.

SUGGESTED READINGS

Benne, Kenneth D.: "Some Philosophic Issues in Adult Education," *Adult Education*, vol. 7, no. 2, Winter 1957, pp.67–82.

Bradford, Leland: "Toward a Philosophy of Adult Education," *Adult Education*, vol. 7, no. 2, Winter 1957, pp.83–93.

Brunner, Jerome S.: *On Knowing*, Atheneum, New York, 1962.

Hass, Glen, Kimball Wiles, and Joseph Bondi (eds.): *Reading in Curriculum*, Allyn and Bacon, Boston, 1970.

Littleford, Michael: "Some Philosophical Assumptions of Humanistic Psychology," *Educational Theory*, vol. 20, no. 3, Summer 1970, pp.229–244.

London, Jack: "Reflections Upon the Relevance of Paulo Freire for American Adult Education," *Convergence*, vol. 6, no. 1, 1973, pp.48–61

CHAPTER 10

Guidelines for Curriculum Approaches

In the previous chapter, we outlined three approaches to curriculum development that are currently followed in continuing education: (1) some adaptation of the Tyler approach, (2) the Freirian approach, and (3) the approach of liberal education. Not surprisingly, those subscribing to any one of these three approaches believe *that* approach to be correct. As we pointed out, each approach has definite advantages. But each also has serious flaws that should cause any curriculum planner to pause before adopting it. None of the three can be adopted uncritically.

In this chapter, we will return to the question raised at the beginning of Chapter 8: What should be taught? We will offer some guidelines to help answer that question within the context of continuing education. Then we will explore guidelines that can be used in selecting an approach to curriculum development in continuing education.

WHAT SHOULD BE TAUGHT

How do we decide what the curriculum should be—that is, what should be taught? What we must do is return to the purposes of continuing education. These purposes can provide the basis for determining the content of the continuing education curriculum.

Earlier we mentioned four broad purposes of continuing education:

1. To help people survive—for example, by providing job training, coping skills for day-to-day living, skills for interpersonal relationships, etc.
2. To help people discover a sense of meaning in their lives by helping them to enjoy personal creativity, satisfaction from excellence, and the benefits of emotional and intellectual discovery.
3. To help people learn how to learn.
4. To help people in a community (society) provide a more humane social, psychological, and physical environment for all its members.

We said that an overall purpose of continuing education was to improve the quality of human life, which means that all four of the purposes mentioned must be dealt with at the same time. One purpose should not be promoted at the expense of the others; there is a need for balance among them.

What do knowledge and curriculum mean in terms of these four purposes? Let's look at them in turn.

Curriculum for Survival

Knowledge means job skills, knowing how to get an auto loan, skills for relating to your spouse and children or coworkers, being able to fill out a job application, knowing how to compete in the marketplace.

Knowledge is "out there." It is constantly on the increase as researchers and scientists develop new ideas, "new survival tools." And curriculum is the organization of this knowledge into courses, workshops, or degree programs that will provide efficient access to this knowledge for those who need it.

How do we decide what a curriculum should offer? One of the several curriculum models adapted from Tyler will provide the answer. By consulting with potential participants and specialists and studying the contemporary society, we can work toward determining the kinds of knowledge that people need to help them survive in our rapidly changing society.

Curriculum for Meaning

Here knowledge is apt to include not only the scientific but also the humanistic—that is, the curriculum will draw on the great wealth of experience expressed in human culture—in literature, the arts, and history.

Knowledge may also be viewed as people's everyday experiences. That is, it stems from the experiences of living, working, and playing; from social relationships; from new adventures and familiar routines.

Knowledge as related to this purpose can be viewed broadly. It encompasses everything from the eternal verities expressed in the great books to the ordinary experiences of everyday life.

Curriculum thus becomes difficult to define, for it includes ways and means of organizing knowledge as we have just defined it. It may mean, from an educational perspective, organizing knowledge into packages—into courses, workshops, and the like—to make it as easy as possible for people to assimilate. It also may mean encouraging people to reflect on their daily experiences in an attempt to derive meaning from them. The curriculum of daily living, for most people, is one of the richest sources of knowledge. This knowledge of day-to-day experience can be mixed with the timeless knowledge preserved and passed on through the ages. The combination of the two types of knowledge can help a person derive meaning that goes beyond day-to-day living and makes personal and real the timeless wisdom of human culture.

Curriculum for Learning to Learn

Knowledge that will contribute to learning how to learn may come from books, from other people, or from experience. What is important is how the knowledge is used.

Curriculum then, is developed by organizing ways in which knowledge may be used to help someone learn how to learn. Curriculum in this sense is a process.

The curriculum for learning how to learn may be focused on problem solving. For instance, the program may help someone learn how to solve various problems faced in life through a process of learning particular kinds of skills. Someone wants to buy a house and knows little about borrowing and lending procedures. By reading; by asking questions of realtors, bankers, or knowledgeable friends; by sifting answers to determine which are credible; by working through the problem of how one goes about borrowing for a new home; it is possible to acquire problem-solving skills through learning. Having learned how to solve one kind of problem has taught the individual how to approach the solution of other problems.

It is also possible to learn how to learn in areas that are not problem-related. Say a person has always wanted to know more about farm barns. There are steps this person can follow—entirely without outside help—that will uncover considerable information about barns. These include learning how to use a library, how to interview people, how to read historical material as well as architectural and engineering material, becoming familiar with the language of barn builders, and so on. Once a person has learned how to learn in areas that are of interest, he or she can then proceed to learn almost anything quite independently. In short, this type of curriculum is largely self-directed.

Curriculum for Helping Communities Provide a More Humane Environment

Knowledge includes psychological, sociological, and political research findings. It includes the experiences of people who have lived and worked in a community as well as everything that relates to the life and operation of the community.

In addition, this type of curriculum includes everything we know and can learn about the process of social change. The curriculum is, then, an approach to community problem solving. It is not predetermined by curriculum planners except insofar as they can provide knowledge of the process of community problem solving.

Much of the knowledge included in community problem solving will be acquired or identified through the process by which a group of citizens works on their community's problems. They may look for knowledge about urban development, health care systems, political structures, or about the community's legislative procedures. The specific kinds of knowledge that are included in the curriculum will depend on the community's problem and how the citizens intend to go about dealing with it. The process—the curriculum—is dynamic. As citizens work on a community problem, they often find that they have to shift direction, change emphasis, involve more or different people, consult specialists, try a tentative solution to see if it works, and then come back to reflect on their experience. No one knows what the curriculum will be at the beginning of such a project. What *is* known is that, as a group, the participants want to work toward making their community a more humane place in which to live.

HOW SHOULD THE CURRICULUM BE PLANNED?

As we argued above, continuing education should focus on four purposes—survival, meaning, learning to learn, and social change. What are the alternative approaches to curriculum development that continuing education might adopt? We see four:

1. Follow one of the three models discussed for each of the purposes. That is, follow the Tyler approach when planning curriculum for survival, follow the liberal education approach when planning for meaning, and follow the Freirian approach when planning for community or social change. Along with all this goes the hope that somehow people will learn how to learn on their own.

2. Try to adapt one of the curriculum models to fit all the purposes. For example, try to change Tyler's approach or the liberal education approach sufficiently that it will address all of the purposes we have indicated.

3. Try to integrate the three curriculum models—Tyler, liberal education, Freire—into one approach that will allow all the purposes to be met.

4. Develop fresh approaches to curriculum development that will focus on all four of the purposes for continuing education.

The first alternative could be followed without too much difficulty. In fact, it is the approach that is now followed by much of the field of continuing education. Large numbers of programs are based on the Tyler model, some programs are based on the liberal education approach, and a few isolated programs are based on some type of Freirian approach.

The major problem with this alternative is that no one continuing education effort strives to meet more than one of the purposes. As we argued earlier, continuing education should include all these purposes. And a given program—say one that is sponsored by a university extension—should include more than a focus on survival or only a focus on liberal education. It should include a program that emphasizes both survival and helping people achieve meanings in their lives while at the same time giving them some skills that will enhance their future learning.

The second alternative, adapting one of the models to fit all the purposes, would seem impossible to achieve. To meet the four purposes we have listed would ask far too much of any one of the four approaches with the possible exception of the Freirian approach. But the Freirian approach, with its emphasis on social change and collective action, would have to be modified to include individualized education for survival, which seems to be a contradiction of the approach itself.

The third alternative, merging the three approaches together, is impossible because the three are based on quite different educational and philosophical assumptions. An attempt to merge the three could at best result in what we are describing as alternative 1—separate approaches for separate purposes.

We are left with the fourth alternative. At the outset of this book, we said it was not our purpose to focus on specific how-to-do-it approaches. Therefore we will not, here, present a new approach to curriculum development for continuing education. We would like to emphasize the need for experimental development of new approaches to curriculum development—approaches that uniquely meet the purposes we have outlined for continuing education. Though we will not offer the details of such curriculum development approaches, we will suggest some criteria that should guide those who want to work in this area.

Criteria for New Approaches to Curriculum Development

1. The approach should have a sound philosophical base—it should be grounded on the belief that human beings are unique in many ways, although they also have much in common with other life forms.
2. The approach should be grounded in a belief that the purpose of continuing education is to enhance the quality of human life—to help people survive,

seek meaning in their lives, learn how to learn, and change communities for more humane living. This approach would help people move beyond where they are now.

3. The approach should be grounded in the belief that knowledge is to be found outside the individual—in books, research journals, computers, and the like. But knowledge can also be arrived at as people reflect on their feelings, beliefs, and experiences.

4. The approach should focus on both individuals and groups as the subjects of learning. That is, it will be oriented toward both individuals and communities.

5. The approach should integrate the theoretical with the practical. It should integrate education for survival with liberal education, social change with individual growth.

6. The approach should provide direction with openness, flexible guidelines but not predetermined steps, suggestions but not rules.

7. The approach should not lose sight of the concept of self-directed learning. It should address the question of curriculum development from the perspective of the self-directed learner. The approach should lend itself to both individuals and groups, so that either individuals or groups can follow the approach with little or no outside direction.

8. The approach should emphasize a philosophy of helping people develop enthusiasm for and love of learning that goes far beyond the solution of day-to-day problems. It should seek to help people move into previously unexplored areas of their lives in previously unimagined ways.

The time is ripe for new approaches—fresh approaches that will help continuing education achieve its purposes. Until new approaches are developed, we shall probably continue to falter and stumble.

SUMMARY

In the previous chapter, we examined various perspectives on the concept of knowledge and approaches to curriculum development. In this chapter, we explored various ways of viewing curriculum from the perspective of continuing education as well as the question of how the curriculum for continuing education should be planned. We concluded that a new approach to curriculum development in continuing education is necessary—one that will be consistent with the overall purpose of continuing education—to enhance the quality of human life. Finally, we offered several guidelines to the development of a new approach to curriculum development.

SECTION V

PROCEDURES FOR CONTINUING EDUCATION

T humbing through the literature of continuing education, one easily finds many references to procedures. Much of this literature attempts to answer the question of how one goes about teaching adults.

Unfortunately, much of the literature in continuing education dealing with procedures does not explore more basic questions such as: How can free and liberating learning and action be enhanced? What should the relationship between teachers and learners be?

In Chapter 11, various problems with procedures are explored, including a discussion of various reasons why educators of adults sometimes emphasize procedures excessively, at the expense of more basic concerns.

The emphasis of Chapter 12 is on developing a rationale for teaching and learning in continuing education. The chapter closes with a list of criteria for guiding the selection of procedures.

CHAPTER 11

Problems with Procedures

Let's begin with a story that will be familiar to many of you. A man decides to take up fishing. He's never done it before, but it sounds like an interesting recreational activity, and restful too. He goes to a sporting goods store, where he invests in both casting and spinning rods. He spends several dollars on lures and other equipment which the salesperson assures him are necessary for modern-day fishing. The fisherman buys a boat and a motor.

On the opening day of fishing season, he drives 100 miles to a lake he heard was good for fishing. He launches his boat and spends the day casting his assortment of lures into the depths of the lake, but with no results. As the sun begins to sink in the west, he has still caught no fish.

As he loads his equipment back into the car, he notices an old man carrying several large fish. The old man carries a fishing rod, but it is an inexpensive one, and he has obviously been fishing from shore.

The well-equipped fisherman doesn't bother to ask the old man how or where he caught the fish. He roars off in his car, wondering what he had done wrong—particularly since he had spent several hundred dollars preparing for this new recreational activity.

What has all this to do with approaches to teaching in continuing education? Think of the well-equipped novice fisherman as an educator of adults who has been seduced by the "procedures syndrome." This educator may know all the tricks of the trade—how to use a variety of audiovisual equipment, large- and small-group techniques, panel discussions, and all the rest. Yet this educator is often less than successful, particularly when the variety of procedures used lacks an adequate rationale.

The old man, who had more modest fishing equipment, knew from experience where the fish could be found. He knew what lures attracted them. He knew how to use his equipment in light of his knowledge about the lake and the fish, and he was more successful. The old man first had a rationale for what he was doing. This rationale served as a basis for his selection and use of the equipment. True, the old man could likely have done even better had he had a boat and motor and equipment that would allow him to cast his lures farther. But it is not primarily the equipment that makes a successful fisherman. It is a basic understanding of lakes, fish, weather, and the hundreds of other factors that influence fishing—as well as some basic attitudes about the sport.

Likewise, it is not a thorough understanding of procedures in continuing education that brings success to an educator of adults but a basic understanding of human beings, of how learning occurs, of viewpoints regarding knowledge and the purposes of continuing education, and of the characteristics of adults as learners. These form the rationale for how one teaches—for the procedures one uses in working with adults.

In this chapter we will explore the reasons why many educators of adults have become so taken with procedures, often without examining the basic rationale for their use. Then we will suggest that this overemphasis on procedures serves to cloud the more important questions that educators of adults should address.

REASONS FOR EMPHASIS ON PROCEDURES

Educators of adults are excessively interested in procedures for many reasons. Here are a few:

Reaction to Schooling

It is only within the last 50 to 75 years that continuing education has begun to flourish in this country. As it began to develop, its pioneers quickly discovered that adults could be educated outside of formal classrooms, with their tightly organized schedules and curricula. They discovered, for instance, that a group of farmers interested in learning about better feeding of dairy cattle could meet in a barn and talk about their own problems. Many of these same farmers could be reached through a newspaper column. Or they could be taught by an educator who would go out to the farms, so that the educator and farmer together, learning over the barnyard fence, could talk about what bothered the farmer.

Educators of adults were free to explore educational procedures other than lectures, recitations, examinations, and homework—everything that was traditionally associated with formal schooling. These educators, many of them at one time teachers at formal schools, suddenly were free to try new approaches—to arrange the chairs in circles rather than in rows, to try a group discussion rather than a lecture, and to place some measure of the responsibility for instruction on the participants themselves.

Unfortunately, some of these neophyte adult educators assumed that if a few new approaches were useful in facilitating learning, then a lot more new approaches would be even more useful. So begin the various enumerations of procedures for teaching adults, which contributed to the publication of Coolie Verner's seminal work *A Conceptual Scheme for the Identification and Classification of Processes for Adult Education.*[1]

In this monograph, Verner developed a system for the classification of methods, techniques, and devices.

Advent of Electrical Gadgetry

Coincidental with the burgeoning of interest in new procedures for teaching adults came the invention of numerous electrical gadgets designed to "enhance" teaching. Slide and movie projectors were on the scene early, but only the most muscular educators could tote these early models around. Later came smaller, more refined models that even the most mechanically inept could operate with some success. The overhead projector came on the scene as the device that would answer every educator's need, particularly those who detested chalk dust on their hands and chalkboards in general.

There followed such devices as flannel boards and flip charts with felt marking pencils. (These obviously weren't electrical, although occasionally educators felt the need to illuminate them with spotlights.)

Soon came the audio recorder (wire at first, and then tape) and then the cassette for those of us with larger-than-normal thumbs who could never thread the tapes properly. And the dreams of the educators soared. Why, it was possible to capture on tape people's voices and then play them back while the individuals heard speaking were many miles away.

The conference telephone enabled several people in a classroom in

[1]Coolie Verner, *A Conceptual Scheme for the Identification and Classification of Processes for Adult Education*, Adult Education Association of the U.S.A., Washington, D.C., 1962.

northern Wisconsin to talk with a celebrity in New York City or perhaps San Francisco.

The advent of refined computer technology provided for many types of educational opportunities, from simulations of reality situations to various kinds of computer-assisted programmed learning projects.

Television and videotape recording opened up new vistas of electrical gadgetry. Now it was possible to capture on tape not only voices but also pictures, which could be stored and played at any time. And if one didn't understand what was being said, it was possible to play it back—several times if necessary—until one did understand.

Today, with the various combinations of computers including television screens and telephones, it is possible to listen to lectures or watch demonstrations in one's home and call in questions to the TV educator on one's telephone.

This new equipment was heavily advertised and promoted. Both teachers and educational administrators were constantly bombarded with information about what was new and how such technology would not only make one's job as a teacher easier but also help the participants learn more and faster. And, it was claimed, such learning would stay with them longer.

Of course, few seemed to give much thought to how this gadgetry would fit within continuing education; therefore we saw evidence of bizarre responses. If one slide projector was a good thing, then three would be three times as effective, particularly if they could be synchronized to turn off and on in rotation. And if three slide projectors were three times as effective as one, would not *many* slide projectors flashing off and on be many times more effective still? Recently we learned of an educator who had devised a slide presentation involving forty-six projectors. "Watch the screen," he said. "Doesn't it look just like a moving picture?"

No one had the heart to point out that one movie projector could have done the same thing.

Different Approaches for Adults

As continuing education began to grow in prominence, several educators of adults began to suggest that adults were not the same as children and therefore could not be taught using the same procedures used for children.

Malcolm Knowles probably did more work in this area than any other educator of adults as he worked to develop andragogy—the process of teaching adults. He contrasts andragogy with pedagogy—the processes used in teaching children.[2]

[2]Malcolm Knowles, *The Modern Practice of Adult Education: Andragogy Versus Pedagogy*, Association Press, New York, 1970.

Assuming that adults were different from children, many educators of adults began searching for those instructional approaches that uniquely fit the adult learning experience.

Many educators assumed that adults would lose interest unless the procedures were "innovative." Some educators took this further and often implicitly assumed that unless adults were entertained, they would cease to participate. So there was (and is) a considerable attempt to select educational procedures that have a high entertainment value. Of course, this approach can backfire.

The story is told of the adult educator who was gimmick-prone and entertainment-oriented. He had set up a bank of three projectors that were synchronized to a tape recorder. He was presenting the topic of agency organization to a group of people who had recently begun work with a given agency. The lights dimmed, the tape recorder clicked on with pleasing background music and the deep voice of a professional narrator, and the slides flashed off and on the screen in a panorama of color and words.

When the half-hour presentation was over, the lights came up and the educator asked, "Are there any questions?" He was prepared to amplify on any subtlety of agency organization. After a few moments of silence, someone from the back of the room raised his hand and asked, "I wonder if you'd take a few minutes to tell us how all that equipment works. . . . I'm sure impressed." The question is still open whether this person learned anything about the organization of the agency.

Testimonial Influence

Another factor which has encouraged educators to attempt new approaches to teaching adults is testimony from those who have tried them.

Without regard to the effectiveness of a particular approach, those who try new things seem inclined to report favorably on their experiences, in the hope that others will follow their example. Perhaps this is as it should be, but often that which didn't work so well is not mentioned or at least is downplayed.

The pressure from one's peers is indeed strong, particularly if it is couched in terms of keeping up to date. The assumption is that as one continually tries new teaching approaches and uses increasingly more complex equipment, he or she is in step with progress.

Ideology of Neutral Education

A more subtle factor which tends to encourage educators to use teaching procedures uncritically is the assumption that education is neutral. That is, education is often viewed narrowly as the passing of information from teacher to student without concern for values. Educators who explicitly or implicitly accept the assumption of the neutrality of education search for ways to transfer information from teacher to student more efficiently. Thus these educators are often quick to adopt new procedures that emphasize efficiency in information transfer, and education is reduced to the manipulation of techniques.

Given our fascination with techniques, external pressures to keep on top of our field, and acceptance of the ideology that education is neutral, it is not surprising that many adopt new teaching techniques uncritically.

ISSUES IN TEACHING AND LEARNING OVERLOOKED

As educators debate which procedures are the least costly, which are most efficient in transferring information, and which are most up to date, other more important issues are often overlooked.

1. How can free and liberating learning and action be enhanced? What might be done to help eliminate the dependency relationship that often develops between teacher and learners? How can people be encouraged to take charge of and assume responsibility for their own learning?
2. What should be the relationship between teacher and learners? How can the teacher, who is often a specialist in a given content area, be brought together with learners in such a way that the teacher facilitates learning rather than imposing his or her point of view? How can the teacher's integrity and special knowledge be recognized in the educational process?
3. If we assume that the educational process is not neutral, what are the implications of this for the educator of adults and for the adult learner?
4. How do our answers to questions 1 through 3 above guide us in our selection of procedures for the education of adults?

SUMMARY

Educators of adults have shown a great interest in adopting new teaching techniques and educational technology. Often these new approaches have been adopted without critical examination and without attention to a basic rationale for accepting or rejecting a particular approach or technology. Some of the reasons suggested for this often uncritical adoption of procedures include (1) a reaction to schooling, (2) the advent of electrical gadgetry, (3) the belief that different approaches are required for adults, (4) testimonial influence, and (5) the ideology that education is neutral.

By spending so much time discussing educational procedures, many educators of adults have overlooked more pressing issues—such as the question of how free and liberating learning and action can be enhanced, what the relationship between teacher and learners should be, and the implications of a nonneutral education for teaching and learning.

Earlier in this chapter, we talked about the need for a rationale for selecting procedures. We said that the rationale should include a basic understanding of (1) human beings, (2) the purposes of continuing education, (3) the characteristics of adults as learners, (4) viewpoints on knowledge, (5) how learning occurs, and (6) how learning may be facilitated. In previous chapters, we have discussed points 1 through 4. In the next chapter, we will explore points 5 and 6.

CHAPTER 12

Developing A Teaching - Learning Rationale

To make decisions about educational procedures and generally to improve the quality of educational experiences for adults, we argue the need for a thoughtfully developed educational rationale. This rationale should include a position on teaching–learning.

In this chapter we will explore learning and learning theories, the concept of teaching, and several guidelines for developing a rationale for procedures in continuing education.

LEARNING AND LEARNING THEORIES
As one reviews the literature of learning, it is not difficult to find as many as ten or fifteen different theories described. Here we will summarize five theories that seem to have application to continuing education: the (1) mental discipline, (2) unfoldment, (3) apperception, (4) behaviorism, and (5) gestalt–field theories.

The two theories that are most commonly debated in continuing education are behaviorism and gestalt–field. Though these may be the popular theories for debate, many educators subscribe to one of the other three theories, either knowingly or unknowingly.

It's an old aphorism that one teaches as one has been taught. Many educators of adults today grew up during a time when mental discipline or, even more likely, apperception were the predominant theories guiding schooling in this country. Thus it is important to discuss these theories if for no other reason than to help people become more conscious of the views that guided their formal education. Of course, there may be more practical reasons for analyzing these "historical" theories. There is always the nagging thought that though they have been around for years, they may yet provide some direction for the problems that today's educator of adults faces.

Classical Mental Discipline

Classical mental discipline focuses attention on developing the powers of reason and, second, stocking the mind with knowledge.

> . . . [The] classical tradition would have us believe that training the mind means developing our implicit powers of reason; and this, in turn, has often come to mean teaching . . . the rule of logical systems on the assumption that such systems represent the proper, correct, and intended use of the mind. And, still on balance, the classical tradition would also have us believe that the mind so trained is disciplined— which is to say that it would, as a consequence, seem to possess the bodies of certain, indubitable, metaphysical knowledges that represent ultimate and absolute truth.[1]

For the classical mental disciplinarian, therefore, learning is a matter of developing the mind. According to Bigge, "learning becomes a process of inner development within which various powers such as imagination, memory, will and thought are cultivated."[2]

The approach of classical mental discipline, in other words, emphasizes developing the logical powers of reason. In fact, the proponents of this theory put a low priority on knowledge that is solely based on empirical evidence.

> Education deals with the development of the intellectual powers of men. . . . [but] we cannot talk about the intellectual powers of men, though we talk about training them, or amusing them, or adapting them, and meeting their immediate needs, unless our philosophy in general tells us that there is knowledge and that there is a difference between true and false. We must believe, too, that there are other means of

[1]Charles J. Brauner and Hobert W. Burns, *Problems in Education and Philosophy*, Prentice-Hall, Englewood Cliffs, N.J., 1965, p. 37.

[2]Morris L. Bigge, *Learning Theories for Teachers*, 3d ed., Harper & Row, New York, 1976, p. 24.

obtaining knowledge, than scientific experimentation. . . . [and] if we are to set about developing the intellectual powers of men through having them acquire knowledge of the most important subject, we have to begin with the proposition that experimentation and empirical data will be of only limited use to us. . . . [3]

The classical mental disciplinarian argues that the knowledge of the truly educated person may not be directly related to any everyday practical use. People who have studied the "great principles" passed down through the ages have developed an approach to reasoning and a stock of knowledge that is important to their very humanity—and this process of reasoning and store of basic knowledge transcends their practical, everyday existence. The classical mental disciplinarians strive to move people beyond the mundane toward the truly human, helping them to discover their ties to both history and culture.

Contemporary proponents of the theory of classical mental discipline include Mortimer J. Adler and Robert M. Hutchins. The great books program developed by these men is an example of a continuing education program based on the principles of classical mental discipline.

Those who advocate this approach to learning are often criticized for being elitist. The literature in many ways would support this criticism, for many advocates of classical mental discipline have concentrated their attention on the wealthy and those who have already achieved high levels of education.

Unfoldment

One way to understand the theory of unfoldment is to think of a tiny, closed rosebud. As it receives sunlight, moisture, and nutrients from the soil, the bud grows larger and slowly opens, revealing all its color and grandeur. From the very beginning, the potential for beauty was present in the tiny bud. All that it needed to develop into a beautiful, unfolded flower was the proper nourishment.

Likewise, each person, as viewed by those who advocate this theory of learning, is seen as having a great potential for growth and development. Education is a means for assisting this person to unfold, to realize this great potential that lies within.

Insofar as knowledge and truth are concerned, the person's "emotional feelings, not his intellectual thoughts, are taken to be the final authority for truth. Hence, he (she) arrives at decisions on all issues in accordance with the way he feels, and he is completely confident that he is right." [4]

[3]Robert M. Hutchins, *The Conflict in Education in Democratic Society*, Harper & Row, New York, 1953.

[4]Bigge, op. cit., p. 33.

Advocates of this learning theory place great stress on the concept of needs and upon the process of growth and development.

When they allude to learning, they seem to assume or imply that it is little more than a process of growth and development in accordance with the genetic patterns of individuals. . . . Needs are considered . . . [person] centered, as contrasted with their being either environment or situation centered. As an organism or mind naturally unfolds through a series of stages, each stage is assumed to have its unique needs. Such . . . [person] centered needs have much in common with instincts, they are innate determining tendencies or permanent trends of human nature that underlie behavior from birth to death under all circumstances in all kinds of societies.[5]

The theory of unfoldment can be traced back to the writings of Jean Jacques Rousseau (1712–1778). Its later proponents included Heinrich Pestalozzi (1746–1827) and Friedrich Froebel (1782–1852). Important contemporary advocates of this approach are Abraham Maslow and Carl Rogers.

Critics of the theory of unfoldment point to its extremely individualistic orientation. Often the learner does not think of history and past culture as things to be learned. The learner is not usually concerned about the larger society and its problems but focuses only on individual needs and concerns. The proponents of this theory fail to consider the fact that many of our needs, feelings, and thoughts are culturally conditioned.

To many, the idea of knowledge as identified with the self is "soft," i.e., too subjective. That is, such knowledge cannot be verified if it is held solely by one person who merely *feels* it to be correct.

Apperception

Apperception is often referred to as Herbartianism, after Johann Friedrich Herbart (1776–1841), who was instrumental in developing the theory. It is based on the assumption that the mind is a tabula rasa (a blank slate) or an empty vessel to be filled with knowledge.

Learning, for those who subscribe to this theory, is the formation of an apperceptive mass. By "apperceptive mass" is meant the aggregate of mental stages that a person has mastered at any given time. Learning, then, means relating new ideas to existing ideas that are already present in the mind.

Apperception, in contrast to both mental discipline and natural unfold-

[5]Ibid.

ment, is a dynamic mental associationism based upon the fundamental premise that there are no innate ideas; everything a person knows comes to him from outside himself. This means that mind is wholly a matter of content—it is a compound of elemental impressions bound together by association and it is formed when subject matter is presented from without and makes certain associations or connections with prior content.[6]

For the educator who strives to follow apperception theory in teaching, several steps in the teaching process are suggested:

1. *Preparation.* During this step the learner is made aware of the subject matter to be learned. If possible, the instructor tries to relate the subject matter to knowledge that he or she believes the students already hold. For example, if the educator of adults is talking about human nutrition, she might make comments about basic food facts of which she believes her audience is already aware.
2. *Presentation.* The instructor presents the new information.
3. *Comparison and abstraction.* During this step, the students relate the new knowledge to knowledge they already hold. The people participating in the session on human nutrition make connections between the new research and the basic food facts they already have. The process of abstraction represents the students' searching for common elements between what they already know and the new information they are receiving.
4. *Generalization.* At this stage the students attempt to name what is common about what they already know on this topic and the new information they are receiving.
5. *Application.* The learner is asked to apply the new information in, for example, a problem situation. Those learning new information about human nutrition could be asked to prepare a week's menu for their families, using what they have learned as a basis for the project.[7]

Of all of the learning theories we will explore, this one continues to be most pervasive throughout formal education at every level, including continuing education programs.

This theory is the basis for lesson plans, usually built around the five steps described above. It also forms the basis for teaching in which teachers follow a series of steps in their presentation of material.

A variant of this approach to teaching—under the title of adoption–diffusion

[6]Ibid., p. 34.

[7]Ibid., pp. 42–43.

theory—has been used widely in the continuing education programs of the cooperative extension service. Upon examination, we notice a close similarity between the steps of the adoption–diffusion theory and those in the apperception approach described above.

Stage 1—Awareness. People become aware that an idea exists, but they lack the details. They may learn of a new idea at a state fair, from the radio or television, or from a friend. But at this stage they are aware only that the new idea exists.

Stage 2—Interest. The person receives factual information about the idea. He or she learns what it is, where it might be used, how others have used it.

Stage 3—Evaluation. At this point the person relates the new idea to previous information already held. The person compares the new with the old and asks such questions as: "Will this new idea work in my situation?" "Is this idea better than the ideas and knowledge I already have on this topic?"

Stage 4—Trial. The person weighs the relative advantages and disadvantages of the new idea and decides to try the new idea on a limited scale. For example, a farmer may learn of a new hybrid corn variety and—after working through the stages outlined above—decides to plant 5 acres of the new hybrid to see how well it grows on his farm.

Stage 5—Adoption. If the trial is successful, the new idea is included and accepted as a part of the knowledge the person holds.[8]

Each stage of the adoption–diffusion theory can be related to similarly numbered steps in the apperception theory.

What are some of the problems with apperception theory? Many educators today cannot accept any theory that sees the mind as an empty space to be filled by teachers. Others criticize the lockstep approach in the five steps for teaching as mechanical, inhumane, and entirely dominated by the teacher, who preplans everything he or she will do when teaching. From a theoretical perspective, this theory is criticized because it does not explain how the original ideas—those with which new ideas are supposed to be associated—come into the mind. How did the first ideas become established?

Behaviorism

The term "behaviorism" is used here to refer to a family of theories growing out of the orientation of stimulus–response conditioning (S–R). Depending on which

---

[8]Lincoln David Kelsey and Cannon Chiles Hearne, *Cooperative Extension Work*, 3d ed., Comstock Publishing Associates, Ithaca, N.Y., 1963, p. 267.

authors one reads, there are a variety of theories subsumed under the title "behaviorism"—such as connectionism, which is often associated with E. L. Thorndike; conditioning with no reinforcement, which is associated with J. B. Watson and E. R. Guthrie; and conditioning with reinforcement, associated with B. F. Skinner and R. M. Gagné.

Our attention here will focus on the so-called neobehaviorists, represented by Skinner and Gagné. To understand neobehaviorism, one must understand the assumptions behind the theory—and the most fundamental of these is that human nature can be explained in essentially mechanistic terms. That is, human behavior is wholly determined and therefore capable, ultimately, of both prediction and control.

Another assumption held by the behaviorists can be labeled "scientific realism."

> Realists have been convinced that the physical world experienced by human beings is real and essentially what it appears to be when observed through the senses. . . . a basic principle of the universe is sequential cause and effect; every event is determined by events that have gone before it. Thus, the universe is a vast mechanism governed by natural laws, which are essentially mechanical in nature. . . . nothing should be asserted to be real or meaningful unless, through observation, it can be subjected to objective study, using only publicly verifiable data. If anything exists, it exists in some amount; if it exists in some amount, it can be measured.[9]

Behavior and learning are inescapably determined by the environment—that is, by influences that originate outside the person.

The neobehaviorists define learning as a more or less permanent change in behavior. "Accordingly, the learning process consists of impressions of new reaction patterns on pliable, passive organisms. . . . the key concepts of neo-Behaviorists are stimuli—excitement provided by an environment—and responses—reactions—made by an organism."[10]

B. F. Skinner's particular application of behaviorism with positive reinforcement is followed by many practitioners of continuing education. Competency-based education is essentially based on a behavioristic model of learning; that is, determine the end behaviors or competencies desired and then design learning experiences that will evoke these intended behaviors in the learners.

Individualized programmed learning also has its roots in behaviorism. Besides its individualized nature, some of the very real advantages to this

[9]Bigge, op. cit., p. 61.
[10]Ibid., p. 86.

educational approach are that (1) feedback and thus reinforcement to the learner is immediate; (2) the individual is active in the process since he or she must respond to each question or situation; (3) the correct answer must be chosen before the reinforcement is provided, thus avoiding the situation of partially correct answers; and (4) the individual is able to work at his or her own rate of speed.[11]

Although there are many applications of behavioristic theory within continuing education, the theory is not without its critics. Indeed, behaviorism is attacked more than the other four approaches combined.

The behaviorists are criticized at various levels. Their basic assumptions are challenged. For example, critics challenge them on their belief that human beings are really no different than animals and can be treated quite mechanistically. Some critics see the emphasis on attempting to change a person's behavior as inhumane. Other critics ask the behaviorists what right they have to attempt to change the behavior of others. Does not behaviorism lead to totalitarian control by a technology-oriented minority?

At the theoretical level, the reductionistic approach taken by the behaviorists also is challenged. The behaviorists assume that the totality of a situation, a subject matter, can be broken into pieces and each piece dealt with in an additive fashion. That is, a person will learn the pieces one at a time with the assumption that when all the pieces have been learned, the individual will "know" the total situation. As we shall see in the next section, the gestalt–field theorists, particularly, challenge reductionism and suggest an opposite viewpoint—that one must begin with the totality of a situation. Whenever the individual is considered as part of the whole, one must see the individual in relation to the totality and to the other parts.

Another challenge to the behaviorists centers on their definition of learning as change in behavior. Green writes, "a change of behavior [is] at best only *evidence* of learning . . . A person may learn to do something and yet never in his life decide to do it or in any way display his knowledge or capacities."[12]

Gestalt–Field Theory

Today, the learning theory that provides the greatest competition to behaviorism is the gestalt–field theory of learning. Proponents of this theoretical orientation to learning include Kurt Lewin, Rollo May, Gordon Allport, John Dewey, Jerome Bruner, Morris Bigge and many others.

[11]Samuel S. Dubin and Morris Okun, "Implications of Learning Theories for Adult Instruction," *Adult Education*, vol. 24, no. 1, pp. 3–19, 1973.

[12]Thomas F. Green, "The Concept of Teaching," in Donald Vandenberg (ed.), *Teaching and Learning,* University of Illinois Press, Urbana, Ill., 1969, p. 10.

Where the behavioristic theories of learning assume scientific realism—sequential cause and effect, mechanical natural laws, and measurability as a test of reality—the gestalt–field theories assume relativism. The central thrust of relativism is that everything is related to everything else, and that a thing's qualities are derived from its relationship to other things.

"Knowledge is a matter of human interpretation, and not a literal description of what exists external to people. . . . Relativists assume that no scientific law is 'sacred'; any law may change, and indeed over the course of time most will. A significant aspect of the thinking of relativists is their expectancy of change."[13]

Within the gestalt–field theoretical orientation, considerable stress is placed on the practical uses of knowledge. For example, Brauner and Burns assert:

> . . . the classical thinkers see the end of intellectual activity, or "acquiring," as the mastery and possession of some fixed, final, antecedently existing body of knowledge that is of intrinsic value; while modern thinkers (Gestalt–field theorists), on the contrary, see the end of intellectual activity, or "inquiring," as the creation and implementation of a well-designed and well-executed plan of action geared to the resolution of some difficulty, some problem—the inquiry, therefore, presupposes that all bodies of knowledge are contingent, relative, and of instrumental value.[14]

In some ways, one may view the gestalt–field theory of learning as a combination of the unfoldment theory, described above, with some aspects of scientific realism—one of the bases of behaviorism. A basic assumption of the gestalt–field approach is interaction or transaction (the word used by John Dewey to describe the interplay between the individual and his or her environment).

> With the emphasis upon interaction, the responsibility for development rests neither with the person alone (as Rousseau would have said) nor with the environment alone (as the scientific realist would say). Instead, it is in a person and his environment coming together in a psychological field that Gestalt–field psychologists find their clue to psychological development and learning.[15]

[13]Bigge, op. cit. pp. 65–66.

[14]Brauner and Burns, op. cit., p. 50.

[15]Bigge, op. cit., p. 67.

In defining learning, the key word for the gestalt–field theorist is "insight." Learning is defined as the process of developing new insights or modifying old ones. An insight occurs when a person discovers a new way to use elements of his or her environment. This usually happens when the person has worked through some difficulty or some problem (experiencing). Insights occur in individuals; that is, insights are always a learner's own.

According to gestalt–field theory—and in contrast with behaviorism—learning is always purposive. A person learns because of some problem situation being faced, some difficulty that must be overcome, some disequilibrium that has arisen. The purpose of learning may be either to achieve something or to avoid something. Thus motivation for the gestalt–field theorist is personalized and a product of a person's interaction with his or her environment.

Some of the critics of gestalt–field theory point out that it is difficult to experience everything directly. History, for example, cannot be experienced directly. Probably one of the most important criticisms relates to the assumption of the gestalt–field theorists that all learning is problem-related. What of the content of the arts and literature? Would these topics be set aside because their relationship to problem solving seems remote?

And at another level, one can criticize gestalt–field theorists who emphasize problem-solving learning in terms of the learner's day-to-day world exclusively. Is it not possible to conceive of people dealing with their everyday problems but also going beyond these problems to develop the potentials that are uniquely human? Consider, for example, our capacities to derive meaning from a variety of situations, the joy of learning for its own sake without any perceived pragmatic value, or experiencing for the sake of the experience—not because it will lead to some problem solution or some utilitarian insight. Does problem solving encompass all human meaning? Is this not another kind of reductionism?

Learning Defined Five Ways

In summary, as we reflect on the five learning theories outlined above, we see that learning is defined in five different ways. To the classical mental disciplinarian, learning is training the mind and accumulating knowledge. It is an inner developmental process that focuses on such powers as imagination, memory, will, and reason.

Those who subscribe to the theory of unfoldment see learning as a process of individual development. This highly individualized learning includes feelings as well as facts. As people unfold or develop throughout life, according to this view, they experience various needs which serve to motivate learning.

Those who support the apperception theory of learning see it as a dynamic process whereby one forms a collection or aggregate of learnings that never remain fixed. The process of learning, according to this theory, means relating new ideas to the existing ideas and facts that are already present in the mind.

For the behaviorists, learning is a change in behavior. This learning or change in behavior is controlled by environmental influences that originate from outside of the learner.

Proponents of gestalt–field theory, on the other hand, define learning as the development of insights resulting from the person's interaction with his or her environment. This interaction or experience is usually characterized as "problem solving."

What all these definitions have in common is change. A person who has learned has changed. The person may have increased his or her store of knowledge, may have developed skills in rational thinking, may have moved toward higher levels of development, may have added to an apperceptive mass, may display changed behavior, or may have gained insight from interaction with his or her environment through a problem-solving experience.

THE CONCEPT OF TEACHING

Now that we have explored several learning theories, we are ready to look at the other side of the teaching–learning equation—teaching. What is teaching from the perspective of the education of adults?

Problems with Terms

At the outset we must deal with a problem that has plagued the field of continuing education from the beginning. What do we call this person who in some way assists with the education of adults? One of the unique characteristics of the field is the variety of people who, in one way or another, assist with education. Cyril O. Houle describes this situation as a pyramid of leadership. At the bottom are the unpaid volunteers—the leaders of discussion groups, the organizers and leaders of church adult education sessions, and the many leaders in the cooperative extension service who assist with youth and with education programs for adults.

At the second level, according to Houle, is a smaller group of people who have primary responsibility in other areas and assist with the education of adults as a secondary activity. These people include librarians; pastors; staff people at museums; members of the military who are in charge of educational programs; personnel officers in business, industry, and government; and people who are employed by the mass media.

At the top of the pyramid, the smallest group comprises those who have primary responsibility for the education of adults.

Table 1

LEARNING THEORIES AND RELATED ASSUMPTIONS

Theory	Assumptions About Humans	Assumptions About Learning	Assumptions About Knowledge
Classical Mental Discipline	Mind can be developed through exercise	Developing the mind	Fixed body of principles handed down—and processes of logical thought
Unfoldment	Potential for personal development	Process of personal development	Individualistic; feelings are as important as facts
Apperception	Mind is blank slate	Formation of associations between new and old ideas, facts	Exists outside the person
Behaviorism	Can be explained in mechanistic terms	Change in behavior	May be broken into parts. Exists outside the person
Gestalt-Field	Purposive-interact with their environment	Problem-solving thus new insights	Relative. Parts must be considered in relation to whole

They include: Those who direct the adult education activities of public schools, universities, libraries, museums, social settlements, prisons, and other institutions; to professors of adult education and others who devote their central attention to training activities in the field; specialists in adult education on the staffs of agencies with particular interests; directors of training in government, industry, or labor unions; and most of the staff of the Cooperative Extension Service.[16]

[16]Cyril O. Houle, "Professional Education for Educators of Adults," *Adult Education*, Spring 1956, p. 133.

Rather commonly, those who constitute the base of the leadership pyramid described by Houle are referred to as volunteer leaders or simply volunteers.

People at the second level present little problem with titles, for they use the title for their primary activity—librarian, pastor, etc.

But what should we call those at the peak of the pyramid? "Teacher" or "instructor" are titles that many educators of adults resist because they seem to imply a formal schooling situation; adult educators want to avoid that connotation when possible. "Educator" to many of these people is too formal. So a variety of titles is used. The cooperative extension service has used the term "agent" for many years. There are agricultural agents, resource development agents, urban agents, and the like. A more generic title used by some is "change agent"—connoting a person who facilitates change. Some educators of adults dislike the term "change agent" because it seems to imply the right of one person to change another.

Other terms used are "facilitator," "guide," and "helper." Those who advocate the unfoldment theory of learning tend to use these terms, for they imply that the educator is not intervening directly but standing on the sidelines ready to assist the learner when assistance is requested. For similar reasons and because of the association of teachers with schools, Paulo Freire preferred to call the teachers of adults in his literary programs "coordinators." (See Chapter 9.)

Some use the term "adult educator." In Chapter 5, we pointed out some of the problems with that term.

What to call the person who has responsibilities for continuing education programs therefore remains a problem, though it is probably magnified to a level of seriousness that it doesn't deserve. More important is the question of what the educator of adults does or should do to enhance learning. We turn, then, to several points of view about the role of the educator of adults.

In the following discussion, we will use the terms "educate" and "teach" as synonymous even though some people make distinctions between them.

A Teaching Continuum

Green deals with teaching as a continuum. He talks about training and conditioning at one end of the continuum and instruction and indoctrination at the other end. For Green, training and conditioning relate to *doing*; instruction and indoctrination relate to *believing*.

Conditioning may be considered a form of teaching which aims at enabling the learner to perform some act without subjecting it to rational analysis. Certain types of behavior modification may be classed as conditioning, where the learner's behavior is changed but no intelligent consideration or choice is involved.

Training also aims to change behavior, to show the learner a different way to do something. But some intelligent consideration of the behavior is a part of the process. For example, people who wish to become ambulance drivers are trained in first aid skills—how to deal with cardiac arrest, broken limbs, and the like. As a part of the training that focuses on their correct response in these critical situations, they are told why certain techniques are required. But the learners in such a training situation do not have the opportunity to decide for themselves, after weighing various data and evidence, which techniques they will use.

Instruction, the third type of teaching, is related to this weighing of evidence. Instruction is "a kind of conversation, the object of which is to give reasons, weigh evidence, justify, explain, conclude. . . ."[17] In *instruction*, then, the learner takes considerable responsibility for wrestling with ideas and making decisions on the basis of information presented.

Indoctrination, at the far end of the continuum, deals with beliefs, as does instruction. As Green asserts: "in proportion as the conversation of instruction is less and less characterized by argument, reasons, objectives, explanations, and so forth, in proportion as it is less and less directed toward an apprehension of truth, it more and more closely resembles what we call indoctrination."[18]

That is, indoctrination also comes to resemble conditioning since no critical use of intelligence is encouraged.

Roles of the Educator

Another way the literature deals with the matter of educating adults is to suggest various roles that might be performed by educators.

Benne, for example, suggests that the educator may be a *model*, an *expert resource*, a *counselor*, or a *guide for the learning process*. In the *model* role, the educator demonstrates through his or her own behavior such things as how to be an independent learner and how to deal with ideas in depth. The educator shows enthusiasm for learning, demonstrates the importance of knowledge in its relationship to life, and so on. Because some learners see the educator as an authority, these learners will often accept the educator as an example.

In the *expert resource* role, the educator functions as one who knows more about the topic being studied than the learners do. This role comes closest to the role of the traditional teacher.

But Benne points out that it may be unrealistic to demand that the educator be an "expert" in a content area.

---

[17]Green, op. cit., pp. 6–8.

[18]Ibid., p. 8.

In an age of super-specialization, it is clearly impossible that a helper [educator] of adults be expert in many fields of knowledge. . . . this may be both an impractical and an unnecessary demand, so far as the helper's [educator's] preparation for any given teaching situation is concerned. Perhaps the better conception of the "expert" function of the helper [educator] is for him to be alive to the need for using the best expertness available, to stimulate learners to seek valid expert knowledge and advice as needed, to require that discussions and investigations designed for adult learning become aware of the limitations in the expertise of the learners, and motivated to seek required expertness as gaps in immediately available knowledge become apparent.[19]

As a *counselor*, an educator of adults focuses attention on the emotional and attitudinal blocks to learning experienced by the learners and also by the educator. A primary activity of the educator of adults who is performing this role is helping adults identify the various barriers to learning and then working toward their elimination. This assumes that there is both a cognitive and an emotional or affective dimension in any learning situation. The cognitive dimension deals with the subject matter or the content to be learned, while the affective or emotional dimension deals with the feelings of participants, the interpersonal relationships among them, and—in general—the dynamics of the learning group.

As a *guide for the learning process*, the educator of adults focuses on the learning process itself and constantly attempts to enhance it. Here the focus is not on what is learned or on what the emotional blocks to learning might be but on the learning process itself. In this role, the educator is responsible for selecting methods—for deciding on approaches that will best facilitate the learning that is planned. Many educators involve the learners in this process, asking them to help make decisions about the steps that they and their peers should take as they work toward achieving their learning goals.

Individual, Group, Community

Another way to view teaching from the perspective of continuing education is to think of it in terms of individual, group, and community.

Boyd and I discuss each of these approaches to learning, identifying them as transactional modes. The term "transactional mode" is used to indicate that in every learning situation there is a transaction, an interplay between the

---

[19]Kenneth D. Benne, "Some Philosophical Issues in Adult Education," *Adult Education*, vol. 7, no. 2, p. 80, Winter 1957.

environment, the individuals, the subject matter, the particular procedures that are used, the learners' goals, and so on.

The individual *transaction mode [exists] . . . when the adult learns by himself, for example, through participation in an independent study course. The adult does not interact with other adult learners, and may not have direct contact with an adult educator. . . . The group transactional mode [exists] . . . when persons meet together, such as in an adult education class to work on some problem or concern they have. There is interaction among the members of the group, and there is opportunity for persons in the group to assist each other in the learning process.*[20]

Boyd and I describe the *community* transactional mode as the learning situation resulting when a group of citizens gather together to work on some community problem they face.

Persons participating in the community problem solving group are vitally concerned about situations outside of their group, indeed the intent of a particular community problem solving group may be to substantially alter some community institution the group feels isn't adequately carrying out its function. The community problem solving group is both influenced by and attempts to influence persons outside of its group.[21]

M. Donald Campbell, in his research, looked at the functions and styles of the educator of adults working within the community transactional mode. He defined "function" as what the educator does and "style" as how he or she does it.

Campbell studied several community problem-solving groups and concluded that the educator functions performed in these groups could be categorized as *internal functions* and *problem-solving functions*. The internal educator functions include:

1. Organizing—helping form a problem-solving group
2. Training—providing instruction on discussion techniques, helping develop leadership from within the group, and teaching a problem-solving process

---

[20]Robert D. Boyd and Jerold W. Apps, "A Conceptual Model of Adult Education," unpublished manuscript, Department of Continuing and Vocational Education, University of Wisconsin—Madison, Madison, Wis., 1977.

[21]Ibid., p. 10.

3. Encouraging—buoying up the group when it needs encouragement
4. Conciliating—dealing with disagreement within the group

The problem-solving functions include:

1. Linking with knowledge
2. Linking with human resources
3. Enlisting support—from the community, from influential citizens
4. Coordinating—coordinating a group's activities with other community groups or governmental bodies

Campbell also identified three educational styles for the educator who works with community problem solving:

1. Information provider—offering technical information and facts about the community
2. Demonstrator—showing how to proceed and sharing what has worked in other situations
3. Facilitator—assisting a problem-solving group to overcome some difficulty it faces; showing concern for both the process of problem solving as well as the outcome[22]

Another approach to individual, group, and community is that of Verner, who refers to these three orientations as methods, in contrast with techniques and devices. Among the individual methods applicable to the education of adults, Verner suggests correspondence study, directed individual study, apprenticeship, and internship.

Correspondence study "is pursued through a variety of techniques usually centered about those of written communication."

Directed individual study "is a relationship . . . established with the learner that involves some direct personal contact between the learner and the agent [educator] so that personal supervision of the learning process can be assured. . . ."

Apprenticeship "is established . . . [when] the learner acquires knowledge and skills through direct participation in learning under immediate personal supervi-

---

[22]M. Donald Campbell, "The Influence of the Adult Educator on Group Growth in Community Problem Solving," unpublished Ph.D. dissertation, University of Wisconsin—Madison, Madison, Wis., 1977.

sion in a situation that approximates the conditions under which the knowledge will be used. . . ."

Internship is "a relationship . . . established so that an individual can have an opportunity, under supervision, to integrate knowledge and skills already acquired through direct participation in a situation similar to that in which such integrated behavior ultimately will apply."[23]

Verner divides group methods into small-group methods and large-group methods. Small-group methods include classes, discussion groups, and laboratories. Large-group methods include assemblies and conventions or conferences. Finally, for Verner, community methods "are those in which the primary orientation is toward the introduction of change and the alteration of behavior patterns within the social system as a unit with changes in individuals and sub-systems presumed to result from changes in the system of which they are a part."[24]

By "techniques," on the other hand, Verner means "the relationship established by the institutional agent (adult educator) to facilitate learning among a particular and precisely defined body of participants in a specific situation."[25]

He then goes on to define techniques in terms of:

1. Those designed to help people acquire information (lecture, panel, forum, symposium, delegates, field trips, and correspondence book lists)
2. Those designed to help people acquire a skill (demonstration, drill, apprenticeship techniques)
3. Those which emphasize the application of knowledge (discussion, internship and committees or workshops)

As distinct from methods and techniques, Verner refers to devices as instructional aids. These he divides into four categories:

1. Illustrative devices—films, slides, posters, and the like
2. Extension devices—radio, television, educational telephone
3. Environmental devices—room and seating arrangements

[23]Coolie Verner, *A Conceptual Scheme for the Identification and Classification of Processes for Adult Education*, Adult Education Association of the U.S.A., Washington, D.C., 1962, p. 14.

[24]Ibid., p. 16.

[25]Ibid., p. 9.

4. Manipulative devices—the tools and equipment learners use to master a particular skill[26]

Those interested in pursuing the topic of methods and techniques further—particularly from the point of view of the variety of methods and techniques and how they can be applied—may refer to the list entitled "Readings on Methods and Techniques" at the end of this chapter.

UNIQUENESS OF ADULT LEARNERS

The question that newcomers to the field of continuing education ask constantly, particularly if they have had experience in formal education with children, is: What do I do differently when working with adults?

As pointed out in Chapter 4, adults are, in many respects, different from children. The aging process affects our sensory ability, our reaction time, and thus the speed with which we can learn. If we believe the various reports of developmental researchers, we can expect adults, as they move through various ages and stages, to experience needs that are different from those of children. We mentioned that adults have the widely recognized if elusive characteristic of maturity, which those who are not yet adult lack.

Along these lines, Zahn notes that

Adults are not merely tall children. They differ from the young in many ways that influence their learning. They have different body characteristics, different learning histories, different reaction times, different attitudes, values, interests, motivations and personalities. Therefore, those who are trying to help adults learn must be aware of these differences and adjust teaching and the learning environment accordingly.[27]

Jean Piaget, who has written extensively about child development, argues that a child's intelligence is not only not as well developed as an adult's but is qualitatively different from adult intelligence. His writing, by implication, suggests that the teaching approaches that are most effective with adults may not always be those best used in teaching children.[28]

Another author who has written a good deal about differences between

---

[26]Coolie Verner and Alan Booth, *Adult Education*, The Center for Applied Research in Education, Inc., Washington, D.C., 1964, pp. 84–86.

[27]Jane C. Zahn, "Differences Between Adults and Youth Affecting Learning," *Adult Education*, Winter 1967, p. 67.

[28]Jean Piaget, *Psychology and Epistemology*, Penguin, Baltimore, 1972.

adult and child learners is Malcolm Knowles. He speaks of self-concept, experience, readiness, and time perspective. As people mature, their self-concept normally changes from that of a dependent personality to that of a self-directed individual. They develop a growing store of experience upon which to draw in learning situations. Their readiness to learn is closely related to their developmental tasks—the age and stage they are in. And as people mature, their learning has more of an immediacy than a postponed dimension to it. Finally, for adults, learning tends to be oriented toward problem solving rather than a particular subject-matter area.[29]

Of course, Knowles is not without his critics. Many writers suggest that some of the "unique approaches" employed by educators of adults have equal application in the education of children. They also insist that children as learners are more like adults than they are different, granting that there are developmental differences such as those discussed by Piaget and that adults have broader experience upon which to draw.

The middle ground on this issue seems to be a recognition that learning is continuous throughout life and that educators should strive to tie together and relate the education which is directed toward young people with that which is directed toward adults. Since today's child is tomorrow's adult, have we prepared the child for a life of learning? On the other hand, have we so divided the education of children and adults that today's child has to begin all over again, when he or she becomes an adult, to learn what learning is and how one goes about it?

TOWARD A RATIONALE FOR CONTINUING EDUCATION PROCEDURES

Up to this point we have explored a number of questions about learning, learning theories, teaching, and teacher roles. We have also outlined approaches to teaching adults, including methods, techniques, and devices. We have tried to confront the question of procedures as they relate to continuing education.

Now we would like to present several criteria designed to assist the educator of adults in making decisions about procedures.

1. *The selection of procedures should be guided by beliefs about the nature of human beings and the adult as a learner.* Earlier in this book we argued for the humanistic approach to understanding human beings. If we accept the humanistic position about human nature, then we must constantly

[29]Malcolm S. Knowles, *The Modern Practice of Adult Education: Andragogy versus Pedagogy*, Association Press, New York, 1970, p. 39.

ask ourselves whether a particular teaching approach we choose violates this basic belief. More specifically:

> *The requirements of growth in the individual rather than the elements of the subject should determine educational method. This places educational process in the individual, who, after all, is the target of change, rather than only in organization of information which may have little relation to the individual. To this basic process of encouraging change can be added specific techniques and methods particularly appropriate to the area of learning and to the type of content. These content-determined techniques, however, will always be secondary to the motivational forces and conditions of human change and growth.*[30]

Paul Bergevin, Dwight Morris, and Robert M. Smith argue:

> *To use adult educational procedures effectively we must be sensitive to the fact that we are working with people—complex persons of flesh and blood—not statistical units or even mere members of a group. All the procedures ever devised will be of little value if we lack sound insights into human nature—our own as well as the other person's.*[31]

We must respect the mutual freedom of educators of adults and adult learners. Selection of procedures should be guided by respect for human freedom and the interactive processes by which people learn.

2. *The selection of procedures should be guided by beliefs about the purposes of continuing education.* We have argued for four basic purposes for continuing education: (*a*) to help people acquire the tools for physical, psychological, and social survival; (*b*) to help people discover a sense of meaning in their lives; (*c*) to help people learn how to learn; and (*d*) to help communities provide a more humane social, psychological, and physical environment for their members. We must keep these purposes in mind and ask if the procedures we plan to select are consistent with them. Or, more specifically, will the procedures we have selected advance the purposes of continuing education?

3. *The selection of procedures should be guided by beliefs about what constitutes knowledge and curriculum.* In Chapter 8, we argued that knowledge comes both from outside the person—that which is found in books and

---

[30]Leland P. Bradford, "Toward a Philosophy of Adult Education," *Adult Education*, vol. 7, no. 2, p. 86, Winter 1957.

[31]Paul Bergevin, Dwight Morris, and Robert M. Smith, *Adult Education Procedures*, Seabury, New York, 1963, p. 4.

other media—and from inside the person—that which is represented by a person's feelings, beliefs, and experiences. In Chapter 9, we said that curriculum is what is taught in continuing education. We described three alternative approaches to curriculum development.

We also argued that any curriculum development process should take into account the self-directed learner who chooses to learn outside the confines of agency or institutional sponsorship. Thus, in our selection of procedures, we need to take into account a broad definition of what knowledge is. We also need to recognize that many learners will not participate in institutional or agency programs but prefer to go it alone. They may, of course, come to the professional educator for suggestions on how best to pursue self-directed learning.

4. *The selection of procedures should be guided by a theory and definition of learning.* According to the five learning theories discussed earlier in this chapter, it is possible to define learning in five different if related ways.

In order to be most consistent with the position we have taken concerning the nature of human beings, the purposes of continuing education, and the nature of knowledge, our definition of learning encompasses a combination of the definitions suggested by the gestalt–field theory and the theory of classical mental discipline. We might call this eclectic theory *gestalt–field—classical theory.*

We have already mentioned the fact that the gestalt–field theory itself combines some elements of the behaviorist theory with some from the theory of unfoldment. Now we want to go one step further and argue the need to include the theory of classical mental discipline as well.

Our primary reason for combining classical mental discipline with the gestalt–field theory is the former's emphasis on more than just problem solving. The approach of classical mental discipline suggests that through a process of learning, people can move beyond their day-to-day existence of mere problem solving—an aspect of life that is so heavily emphasized by writers who subscribe to the gestalt–field approach to learning. The classical mental disciplinarians are interested in helping people move beyond survival to increasingly higher levels of human growth and living.

But people living in today's society are also vitally concerned with survival. Thus our approach to learning must include helping them to acquire survival skills—learning how to get and keep jobs, to relate with other people, to deal with an increasingly complex society, and so on.

A selection of procedures should then be guided by definitions of learning that are based on two major goals: (1) the development of such inner powers of the mind as imagination, memory, will, and reason (classical mental discipline) and (2) the development of insights through the individual's interaction with his or her environment (gestalt–field).

5. *Our selection of procedures should be guided by a view of where learning occurs.* As we pointed out earlier, people may learn by acting alone, in groups, or in community settings. We must be guided by the fact that much learning occurs outside institutional settings as well as within them, that much adult-related education occurs in and through institutions that do not have education as their primary purpose—such as radio and television, churches, labor unions, and business and industry.

> *Because our thinking about learning has been dominated for so long by the image of the school, we know virtually nothing about the potentialities for truly individual learning, or about how the other institutions of society can become adjuncts to and resources for the learning process . . . the problem of education today cannot be solved by schools and colleges. There is too much to know and understand—not just from books, but from conditions, from life, from love and struggle.*[32]

SUMMARY

Focusing on the development of a rationale for the selection and use of procedures, we briefly summarized five theories of learning and the definition of learning related to each. The five theories discussed were classical mental discipline, unfoldment, apperception, behaviorism, and the gestalt–field theory.

The concept of teaching in continuing education was reviewed, with special attention to the problem with terms. Two views of teaching were presented: teaching as a continuum and teaching in terms of the educator's various possible roles. That is, the educator may serve as model, expert resource, counselor, and guide for the learning process.

Various procedures were discussed from the perspective of the individual, the group, and the community.

The topic of the uniqueness of the adult as a learner was explored, and the works of several authors were cited.

Finally, we discussed aids to the educator of adults in developing a rationale for the selection and use of procedures. These aids were presented in the form of five criteria:

1. The selection of procedures should be guided by beliefs about the nature of the human being and the adult as a learner.
2. The selection of procedures should be guided by beliefs about the purposes of continuing education.

[32]Ronald Gross, "After Deschooling, Free Learning," in *After Deschooling What?* Perennial Library, Harper & Row, New York, 1973, pp. 158–159.

3. The selection of procedures should be guided by beliefs about the nature of knowledge and curriculum.
4. The selection of procedures should be guided by a theory and definition of learning.
5. The selection of procedures should be guided by a view of where learning occurs.

SUGGESTED READINGS

Battle, J. A., and Robert L. Shannon: *The New Idea in Education*, 2d ed., Harper & Row, New York, 1974.

Dale, Edgar: *Building a Learning Environment*, Phi Delta Kappa, Bloomington, Ind., 1972.

Grabowski, Stanley M. (ed.): *Adult Learning and Instruction*, ERIC Clearinghouse on Adult Education, Syracuse, N.Y., 1970.

Hiemstra, Roger: *Lifelong Learning,* Professional Educators Publications, Lincoln, Nebr., 1976.

Kidd, J. Roby: *How Adults Learn*, 2d ed., Association Press, New York, 1973.

Knox, Alan B.: *Adult Development and Learning*, Jossey-Bass, San Francisco, 1977.

Miller, Harry L.: *Teaching and Learning in Adult Education*, Macmillan, New York, 1964.

Rogers, Carl R.: *Freedom to Learn*, Merrill, Columbus, 1969.

———: *Putting Knowledge to Use: A Distillation of the Literature Regarding Knowledge Transfer and Change,* Human Interaction Institute and National Institute of Mental Health, Los Angeles and Rockville, Md., 1976.

———: *Theories of Learning and Instruction*, Sixty-third Yearbook of the National Society for the Study of Education, The National Society for the Study of Education, Chicago, 1964.

Vandenberg, Donald (ed.): *Teaching and Learning*, University of Illinois Press, Urbana, Ill., 1969.

Readings on Methods and Techniques

Aker, George F.: *Adult Education Procedures, Methods and Techniques*, The Library of Continuing Education, Syracuse, N.Y., 1965.

Apps, Jerold W.: *How to Improve Adult Education in Your Church*, Augsburg, Minneapolis, 1972.

———:*Ideas for Better Church Meetings*, Augsburg, Minneapolis, 1975.

Bergevin, Paul, Dwight Morris, and Robert M. Smith: *Adult Education Procedures*, Seabury, New York, 1963.

Cathcart, Robert S., and Larry A Samovar: *Small Group Communication: A Reader*, 2d ed., William C. Brown, Dubuque, Iowa, 1974.

Knowles, Malcolm: *Self-Directed Learning*, Association Press, New York, 1975.

Maier, Norman R. F.: *Problem Solving Discussions and Conferences*, McGraw-Hill, New York, 1963.

Minor, Harold D. (ed.): *Creative Procedures for Adult Groups*, Abingdon, Nashville, Tenn., 1968.

Warren, Virginia B. (ed.): *The Second Treasury of Techniques for Teaching Adults*, National Association for Public Continuing and Adult Education, Washington, D.C., 1970.

SECTION VI

DISCOVERING NEW KNOWLEDGE

T he question of how one goes about doing research in continuing education is not a new one. Yet the answers to this question are not only unclear but often in dispute. On the one hand are those who say that continuing education should adopt as closely as possible the research approaches developed and practiced by natural scientists. On the other hand are those who argue for different research approaches more appropriate to the field of continuing education.

The question of research approaches and related problems is discussed in Chapter 13. In Chapter 14, we give several guidelines designed to aid those who are interested in developing new research approaches for continuing education.

CHAPTER 13

Problems With Research

What problems in research do we confront? An immediate response usually includes insufficient funds, too little time to do research, and a shortage of people interested in working on research projects.

Although these problems do exist and are important, there are other, more fundamental problems which we will examine below.

The major problem confronting those concerned about research in continuing education is a contradiction between the predominant research approach and the predominant practice in the field. That is, there is a contradiction between the way in which we carry out educational programs and the way we conduct research in continuing education.

In this chapter we will begin with a description of the prevalent research approach followed by researchers in continuing education, noting the assumptions that undergird this approach. Next we will examine the contradictions between this prevalent research approach and commonly accepted programming practice in the field. Last, we offer several reasons why the predominant research approach continues to be predominant, despite the contradictions.

RESEARCH IN CONTINUING EDUCATION

Within the field of continuing education, four approaches to research are commonly followed. These involve some type of experimental or quasiexperimental design, a comparative case study approach, participant observation, or the survey approach.[1] By far the most common is the survey approach.

In the survey approach, the following sequence of steps is generally followed:

1. Define the research problem. The researcher may derive a research problem from the topics suggested for further research in literature of the field. Or the researcher may find a research problem suggested by some theory he or she finds interesting. The researcher may find a research problem as he or she reflects upon practical experiences in the field.
2. Write objectives and hypotheses. If the researcher follows a classic approach, the hypotheses are written in the null form and the research attempts to falsify them.[2]
3. Develop an instrument. This is usually a questionnaire which is mailed or filled out during an interview either in person or over the telephone.
4. Collect the data. The instrument developed in step 3 serves as the tool for this.
5. Analyze the data. The researcher usually uses a computer to organize the data, figure percentages, print tables, and subject the data to a variety of statistical tests depending on their nature, the hypotheses to be tested, and the wishes of the researcher.
6. Interpret the data in light of the research problem, the hypotheses, and similar research on the same topic. If the classic approach is used, attempt to falsify the hypotheses.
7. Examine the implications of the research, speculating on where the research results might be applied.
8. Suggest topics for further research, including some confession about the inadequacies of the research just completed.

---

[1]See the following for details on how to carry out these research approaches:
Donald T. Campbell and Julian C. Stanley, *Experimental and Quasi-Experimental Designs for Research*, Rand McNally, Chicago, 1963.
Earl R. Babbie, *Survey Research Methods*, Wadsworth, Belmont, Calif., 1973.
Norman K. Denzin (ed.), *Sociological Methods: A Sourcebook*, Aldine, Chicago, 1970.
H. W. Smith, *Strategies of Social Research*, Prentice-Hall, Englewood Cliffs, N.J., 1975.
Paul D. Leedy, *Practical Research: Planning and Design*, Macmillan, New York, 1974.
Deobold B. Van Dalen, *Understanding Educational Research: An Introduction*, 3d ed., McGraw-Hill, New York, 1973.

[2]See Karl R. Popper, *The Logic of Scientific Discovery*, Harper & Row, New York, 1959, 1968, and *Conjectures and Refutations: The Growth of Scientific Knowledge*, Harper & Row, New York, 1963, 1965.

ASSUMPTIONS OF CONTINUING EDUCATION RESEARCH

One way to begin to understand the predominant research approach we have described is to determine the assumptions that guide it. Below is a review of the underlying assumptions about human beings, knowledge, the relationship of the researcher to the researched, and the purposes for research.

Assumptions about Human Beings

Implicit in this approach to research appear to be several assumptions about the characteristics of human beings.

1. Human life is determined—that is human life is essentially a closed system that offers little room for initiative. This assumption follows from the position that human beings are no more than higher-level animals. As we suggested in Chapter 3, there are two basic views of human beings as no more than higher-level animals: the organismic view assumes that human behavior is determined by instinctual drives, while the mechanistic view assumes that human behavior is determined entirely by the external environment.

The implication of the assumption that human life represents a closed system is that it is possible to discover the factors that influence human behavior and, once this is done, to make predictions of human behavior based upon indicators of the amount, type, and direction of influence.

2. People are more similar to each other than they are different. It follows, then, that it is possible to discover, through research, common factors that can serve as generalizations about large groups of people.

3. Unless they are highly trained, people do not have the competency to conduct research. Likewise, people are often inadequately aware of themselves and their circumstances and cannot communicate their needs and problems to others. A highly trained researcher is necessary to discover the realities of life for many people.

Assumptions about Knowledge

Following are several of the assumptions about knowledge that appear to guide researchers who follow the predominant research approach suggested above.

1. We live in a knowable world, which has an objective reality not the creation of the human mind. Knowledge is out there awaiting human discovery.

2. Knowledge is discovered principally through empirical means, that is, through sensory experience. If one can't see, smell, touch, or hear something, its existence is questionable. This sensory experience is guided by human reasoning, which gives it order and direction. And there is a close

relationship between reasoning and sensing, the order to what one has sensed being provided through a process of reasoning.

3. The validity of knowledge is based on repeatability. That which is capable of being "measured" repeatedly with comparable results is assumed to be valid knowledge. For example, a questionnaire may be administered to a random sample of people at a given time and to another random sample of the same group some time later. If in each case similar results are found, the results are deemed valid.

4. Knowledge is measurable and usually convertible to numbers. The converse holds true: that which is not quantifiable is not significant knowledge.

5. Knowledge occurs in patterns. Objects and events in the world are marked by likenesses. Because there are likenesses, it is possible to classify knowledge according to essential properties, functions, or structures. People may be grouped by sex, age, motivations for learning, and cultural background. By classifying such characteristics, the researcher organizes masses of information into patterns or structures that can be communicated to others. Such classifications also lend themselves to various kinds of manipulation for research purposes.

6. Objects, events, and people do not appreciably change their basic characteristics over time. Though objects, events, and people are not totally unchanging, they remain substantially unchanged over the years. This allows researchers to draw generalizations with some assurance that the generalizations will hold for some time.[3]

7. Objects and events may be broken into discrete parts; it is possible to study these discrete parts in isolation from each other and in isolation from the whole of which they are parts. Further, it is assumed that what is discovered in studying the discrete parts can be added together to provide an understanding of the whole from which the parts were originally derived.

Relationship of Researcher to the Researched

Inherent in the approaches followed by the majority of researchers in continuing education are several assumptions concerning the relationship of the researcher to the researched.

[3]See Deobold B. Van Dalen, *Understanding Educational Research*, McGraw-Hill, New York, 1973, pp. 19–23, for a further discussion of the assumptions of what he calls natural kinds and constancy. He also discusses determinism, or cause and effect, as a necessary assumption of research. But many continuing education researchers, even those who follow experimental approaches, seldom assume a cause-and-effect relationship. They are much more likely to speak in terms of relationships such as correlations between variables than in terms of one variable causing another.

1. The researched is an object for study, and the object does not directly participate in the research. It matters not whether what is researched is a human being or a block of coal, each is treated as an object for study. The researcher assumes that it is important to maintain distance from that which is researched in order to maintain objectivity.
2. The situation that exists between researcher and the researched is objective and value-free.
3. Only the researcher has responsibility for discovering knowledge.
4. Because of formal training and experience, the researcher is profoundly more qualified than the researched to discover knowledge.

Purposes of Research

The research approaches suggested above assume some of the following purposes of research:

1. Knowledge obtained from research can be valuable for decision makers who must decide on such matters as what continuing education programs should be offered to which groups, how resources should be allocated, and the like.
2. The researcher adds to a body of knowledge for the field and communicates this body of knowledge widely to those who practice continuing education, to other researchers, and to the public in general.
3. Particularly for those working in university situations, research provides an avenue for promotion to tenure and provides opportunities for recognition and salary increases.

CONTRADICTIONS BETWEEN RESEARCH AND PRACTICE

When the assumptions of the predominant research approach in continuing education are examined, it is not difficult to find many of them in conflict with the assumptions that guide practice in the field. Some of these are outlined below:

1. Continuing education writers such as Knowles, Kidd, and Houle advocate continuing education programs based on the needs of adults. Their writings emphasize that continuing education programmers should consult with adult learners directly to discover what their needs are. An implicit assumption of the common research approaches is that adults cannot know their own needs, their own realities. A researcher examines them and on this basis determines their reality for them. The adults are not involved in the process except for being asked to fill in the blanks on a questionnaire or to answer preplanned interview questions.

2. Continuing education programmers proclaim the importance of treating adults as mature, unique individuals, each different from every other. Research assumes that adults are more similar to than different from one another.

3. Continuing education programmers stress the self-directed nature of adult learning. Research assumes that the behavior of adults is largely predetermined and that they have little capacity for initiative.

We could go on to examine other contradictions between practice and research. For example, there is the issue of whether or not adults should be treated holistically: practice says yes, research assumes no. We could examine the relationship of the educator to the learner versus the relationship of the researcher to the researched. Practice says we should work with people as partners, listening to them and accepting their experience as a valuable contribution to the total learning process. The predominant research approach suggests that we should treat people as objects for study and that, except as targets of research, they should not participate directly in the research process.

But a more important question to pursue at this point is why there are these contradictions in assumptions between the practice in the field and the common approaches to research. (In recognizing the wide range of practice as well as the wide range of research, it should be added that not all practice contradicts all research. Those educators who follow a behavioristic approach to continuing education, for example, are probably not in conflict with the prevailing research approaches.) The question then is: Why do researchers in continuing education continue to advocate a research approach that appears at every turn to be in conflict with much commonly accepted practice in the field?

REASONS FOR THE CURRENT RESEARCH APPROACH

A major influence on research in continuing education is the research that is conducted in the natural sciences. (Some would argue that continuing education is most influenced by social science research. But an examination of social science research shows that *it* is influenced considerably by natural science research—thus the influence on continuing education is really natural science research.)

Like other new fields of study, continuing education as a field of practice and inquiry has felt the need to associate itself with the natural sciences not only for the prestige of association but because of the established success of the natural sciences. Without question, the natural sciences—with their related technical applications—have commanded considerable respect in our society. Natural science research has worked toward solving many of the practical problems which confront us in such areas as health, transportation, and communication. It follows with apparent logic, then, that if continuing education has any hope of becoming equally successful, it must follow the lead taken by the natural sciences.

Not only the question of prestige but also the question of funding is involved. Most of those in positions to make decisions about who should and who should not be awarded research dollars have a natural science research orientation. If planned research does not follow the rigor of a natural science research approach, it is usually not funded.

Likewise, the training of researchers in continuing education is influenced greatly by the natural science approach. Only in the last few years have any attempts been made to suggest research approaches that begin to broaden the rather narrow approaches to research advocated by most natural scientists. These attempts have often met with severe criticism from those researchers in continuing education who rigidly follow the assumptions of natural science research.

At an even deeper level, continuing education research is influenced by a society that puts considerable stress on those things that are easily measured and on technical accomplishment; it tends to regard human beings as objects, much as it regards its various manufactured products. To categorize and measure human beings and their behavior, it is far more comfortable to assume that they are no more than advanced animals. With this assumption, it is possible to work toward increasingly more sophisticated counting and measuring instruments and computerized, statistical manipulation of the results. It is possible to believe that in time, as more sophisticated instruments and research techniques are developed, human beings will be fully understood and their behavior totally predictable.

Of course there are many people who totally disagree with these assumptions about human beings in our society. These people argue that there are human characteristics which cannot be researched in the traditional ways of natural science. Indeed, the very characteristics that make us human are those that do not lend themselves to methods patterned after the natural sciences. As Schumacher has said, those who, in studying people, attempt to follow the research approaches of natural science "leave all the questions that really matter unanswered; more than that, they deny the validity of the questions."[4]

When researchers in continuing education follow the research methods employed by natural scientists, these researchers are limited to those aspects of the human condition with which the tools of natural science can deal. Left behind are those questions that deal with the uniqueness of human beings. As Joseph Wood Krutch says: "we have been deluded by the fact that the methods employed for the study of man have been for the most part those originally devised for the study of machines or the study of rats, and are capable,

[4]E. F. Schumacher, *A Guide for the Perplexed*, Harper & Row, New York, 1977, p. 4.

therefore, of detecting and measuring only those characteristics which the three do have in common."[5]

Researchers who attempt to research the clearly human questions are often accused of doing "soft" research or not doing research at all. The researcher concerned with the unique characteristics of adults is under great pressure to study only those aspects of human life that extend into the realm of animal life in general—many biological questions, for example. To research questions that are clearly and only human in origin takes a pioneering type of researcher who is able to take great risks, and such a researcher is faced with developing entirely new approaches.

SUMMARY

This chapter describes the predominant research approach in continuing education. The steps in this approach generally include defining the research problems; formulating hypotheses; collecting, analyzing, and interpreting data in light of the problem and hypotheses; drafting conclusions; and deriving implications for the field.

This predominant research approach was analyzed according to its assumptions about (1) human beings, (2) knowledge, (3) relationship of the researcher to the researched, and (4) purposes of research.

The predominant research approach was compared with the commonly accepted practice in the field, and several contradictions were highlighted.

Finally, several reasons were suggested why those in the field of continuing education continue to carry out research which imitates that of the natural sciences, even in light of the contradictions between research and practice.

SUGGESTED READINGS

Beveridge, W. I. B.: *The Art of Scientific Investigation*, Vintage, New York, 1957.

Hall, Budd L.: *Creating Knowledge: Breaking the Monopoly*, International Council for Adult Education, Toronto (no date).

Kaplan, Abraham: *The Conduct of Inquiry*, Chandler, San Francisco, 1964.

Kuhn, Thomas S.: *The Structure of Scientific Revolution*, University of Chicago Press, Chicago, 1962.

Pilsworth, Michael, and Ralph Ruddock: "Some Criticisms of Survey Research Methods in Adult Education," *Convergence*, vol. 8, no. 2, pp. 25–33.

Siegfried, Robert: "Science and Technology: Hero of the Past, Villain of the Future?" *Wisconsin Academy Review*, vol. 21, number 3, Summer 1975.

[5]Joseph Wood Krutch, *The Measure of Man*, Bobbs-Merrill, New York, 1954. p. 32.

CHAPTER 14

Approaches To Research

Given the several problems outlined in the previous chapter, particularly the contradictions between the commonly accepted programming practice and the predominant research approach, what alternatives might be suggested? What approaches might be adopted by researchers in continuing education without contradicting the commonly accepted practices?

In this chapter, we will outline several guidelines that may be used in designing new approaches to research in continuing education—approaches that are consistent with practice.

GUIDELINES FOR ALTERNATIVE APPROACHES TO RESEARCH

1. *Knowledge does not exist apart from values.* Researchers are constantly influenced by their traditions, environments, and personalities. As Myrdal says, "Questions must be asked before answers can be given. The questions are all expressions of our interest in the world; they are at bottom valuations."[1]

The idea that it is possible to do purely objective, value-free research is a

[1]Gunnar Myrdal, *Objectivity in Social Research*, Pantheon, New York, 1969, p. 9.

myth. From the very beginning of any research effort, from the time when we first select a subject for inquiry or ask a question, that subject or question—as Myrdal points out—is influenced by our values.

2. *Researchers should examine their research in light of their assumptions and should make these assumptions explicit.* This guideline follows number 1 above. Realizing that research is not totally objective and value-free, researchers should make explicit those assumptions that guide their research. But, as Myrdal cautions, "value premises cannot be entirely a priori, independent of research. Research should start by giving attention to some value premises which it would seem appropriate to utilize, but it must be prepared to adjust these continually."[2]

3. *Research in continuing education should further the purposes of the field of continuing education.* Earlier in this book we argued that the overall purpose of continuing education should be to improve the quality of human life. The subpurposes enumerated were: (a) to help people acquire the tools for physical, psychological, and social survival; (b) to help people discover a sense of meaning in their lives; (c) to help people learn how to learn; and (d) to help communities (society) provide a more humane social, psychological, and physical environment for their members. We argued that in attempting to achieve these purposes, continuing education must seek balance among them: human beings, their social relations, and their environments must be treated as wholes.

Occasionally researchers in continuing education have lost sight of the goal of their research. They have seen it as a way of adding to their personal prestige and advancement or to the prestige of the institution that supported it. Since there is so much stress on publishing research and thus on the advancement of personal careers in continuing education, the adult learner is often overlooked. If included as a "target audience" for the research, the adult learner is seen no differently than any other research "consumer." The mentality is essentially one of production and consumption. The researcher produces something—a product—and the adult learner (along with others such as teachers, administrators, and the like) is the potential consumer of the product. The question raised here is: Does this producer–consumer orientation to research serve to further the purposes of the field?

4. *Research in continuing education should involve the researched (the adult learner) as a subject in the process, not as an object to be studied from a distance.* In an attempt to emulate the natural sciences, many researchers in continuing education have accepted the research style of the natural scientist. That is, the researcher probes, measures, weighs, and otherwise "researches"

---

[2]Ibid., p. 64.

the object of the research, but the researched (object) makes no direct contribution to the process.

By involving the researched in the research process, we take quite an opposite approach. The researcher and the researched become partners in the process of discovering knowledge. The people being studied have a say not only in what problems are to be researched but in the ways the research is to be conducted. The people researched often assist directly in the collection of data—whether it be objective or subjective, quantitative or qualitative. In this way the researcher and the researched are more likely to discover an accurate reflection of the real situation, as opposed to the often inaccurate picture discovered when the researcher treats the researched as an object.

For example, let's look at what often happens when a questionnaire is used in survey research. The respondent is asked to respond in a *forced-choice* situation, checking such answers as "always," "almost always," "sometimes," "almost never," and "never" to a question about how often the person did something. Frequently, the respondent would like to reply, "That isn't the question that applies to me." But there is no opportunity for such a response; the person checks one of the choices and goes on to the next question intent on finishing the exercise so that she or he can get on to more important matters.

It is assumed here that people have the potential for becoming aware of their reality and for communicating this reality to themselves and to others. This point of view is suggested in George Herbert Mead's conception of meaning:

There are two characters which belong to that which we term meanings; one is participation and the other is communicability. Meaning can arise only insofar as some phase of the act which the individual is arousing in the other can be aroused in himself. There is always to this extent participation. And the result of this participation is communicability, i.e., the individual can indicate to himself what he indicates to others.[3]

This is not to say that people are always immediately aware of their reality or even that they can always perceive their reality accurately. Here is where the process of research comes in. By working with the researched as a partner in the process, the researcher can establish what Freire refers to as a dialogical relationship. This dialogical relationship can have as one of its purposes consciousness raising or assisting the researcher and the researched to become aware of elements in the research situation that were not evident prior to beginning the research. This could mean a new consciousness of the nature

[3]Quoted in Anselm Strauss (ed.), *The Social Psychology of George Herbert Mead*, Phoenix Books, The University of Chicago Press, Chicago, 1956, p. 183.

of the problem to be researched and new questions to be addressed. It could also mean answers to the question that were not immediately evident but became evident after dialogue (or shared reflection), data collection, and more dialogue.

5. *Research in continuing education should be of assistance to those researched and at the same time have the potential for adding to a body of knowledge.* Research in continuing education should be practical and of some immediate assistance to those who are involved in the process of research. At the same time, however, the knowledge obtained should have the potential for future application in the field and should contribute to an understanding of the field. Knowledge obtained from research should at the same time be both practical and theoretical.

Practical and theoretical issues are sometimes discussed in terms of basic (theoretical) and applied (practical) research. By "basic research" we mean:

Research conducted for the purpose of developing scientific theories or the basic principles of a discipline, rather than for the purpose of solving some immediate problem. Basic research, of course, lays the essential foundations for applied research. . . . [Applied research is] research directed to the formulation or discovery of scientific principles that can be used to solve some practical problem of business, government, labor unions, etc.[4]

Sometimes theoretical and applied research are viewed as opposing each other. We suggest that attempts should be made to keep theoretical and practical research linked. In any situation where research is being done, both the practical outcomes and the theoretical aspects of that research should be explored. It will be futile to hope that a field of continuing education will ever develop if all the research that is done is strictly applied research. Likewise, if we strive to carry out only theoretical research and avoid the question of its application to the researched, we are violating several of the guidelines we have already suggested. Furthermore, in some sense sound theory can only be known to the degree that it is applied and tested in actual situations.

6. *The practice of continuing education and continuing education research should always be linked.* When we follow the natural science model for carrying out research, the tendency is to view the research situation as a special one. We set up research situations apart from the situations in which people live and work and interact with each other. We bring them question-

---

[4]George A. Theodorson and Achilles G. Theodorson, *Modern Dictionary of Sociology*, Crowell, New York, 1969, p. 347.

naires or contrive special experimental situations—we establish an artificial situation for the purpose of the research.

We suggest that the situations in which people ordinarily find themselves can also at the same time be research situations. For example, an educator working with a group of citizens intent on solving some community problem can assist the group not only in *practical* ways—developing problem-solving strategies, helping them find resources, perhaps helping them with some of the internal problems many groups face—but also in others that are *theoretical*, as in helping the group to reflect on these problems. The reflection process itself, if our minds are open to it, can be viewed as an appropriate aspect of research.

The educator and the group members together are doing at least three things. First, they are participating in problem solving, seeking to work out some solution or at least to alleviate some problem their community is facing. Second, they are participating in a learning activity. They are learning a good deal about their community, its citizens, the power structure, and so on. They are learning something about a process for problem solving and group interactions in this process. Third, they are participating in a research project, attempting to answer such questions as how one deals with seemingly unbending power structures, how one organizes for effective action, and how one deals with internal group problems—such as conflict that may tear the group apart from the inside. Together, the group members and the educator are partners in all this. The results of the research should be of immediate assistance to the group and its situation. But the results of the research effort should also have the potential for application to like groups in other, similar situations. The research is thus, at the same time, both theoretical and practical.

7. *Research in continuing education should view knowledge broadly.* Acceptable knowledge for the researcher in continuing education should be qualitative as well as quantitative. That is, knowledge can be expressed in quantifiable forms, but it can also be expressed in qualitative forms such as statements of value judgments from the people involved in the research process. These quotations may not be quantifiable and thus would not be expressed in numbers. We should not try to force all data into a pattern of numbers and categories, for by so doing we often lose the unique and individual insight of which each person is capable.

Continuing education researchers should be open to knowledge derived from deductive reasoning, from empirical research, and from intuition. At present, natural science research stresses rational–empirical knowledge—that knowledge which is obtained from sensory measurement approaches and which is guided by preplanned questions derived from existing theories.

Knowledge should include the rational–empirical but it should also include the intuitive—that which is subjective in nature and defies measurement but which perhaps is the major source of new associations and breakthroughs in knowledge.

RATIONAL–EMPIRICAL AND INTUITIVE KNOWLEDGE

In our society we tend to separate those concerned with rational–empirical knowledge from those concerned with intuitive knowledge. We sometimes call one group scientists and the other group artists. We find it difficult or impossible to combine into one totality the knowledge that the scientists and the artists glean.

Part of the difficulty in bringing together knowledge from both scientist and artist has to do with the extreme positions some of their exponents take. That is, some scientists take an extremely narrow position, adhering to tightly drawn assumptions about knowledge that serve to discount, by definition, the possibility that intuitive knowledge exists. And likewise, a growing group of people interested in intuitive knowledge—in reaction to what are seen as the constraints of rational–empirical approaches to knowledge—rejects all that science standsffor.

As Ornstein points out:

We find . . . a large group of productive men and women, who might draw from and contribute to an extended understanding of human nature, closed off from it by the strengths of their cultural training . . . [narrow scientism] . . . and a second group all too eager to be told that "life is an illusion" and to join up here and climb aboard the next Kosmik Union Special, flying saucer, or Guru-of-the-Month Club.[5]

Is it not more realistic, however, to believe that the scientist can combine rational–empirical knowledge with intuitive knowledge? And is it not also equally realistic to believe that the artist can combine rational–empirical knowledge with intuitive knowledge?

Because many of us have already had considerable experience with rational–empirical knowledge and have been trained in its use, and because the very idea of utilizing intuitive knowledge in research may be new, let's look in some depth at intuitive knowledge.

Intuitive Knowledge

Like so many phrases used in the social sciences, "intuitive knowledge" has several meanings.

[5]Robert E. Ornstein, *The Mind Field*, Pocket Books, New York, 1976, pp. 22–23.

Intuitive knowledge for some is knowledge that comes from grasping the relationship of the parts to the whole and the relationship of the parts to each other.

Let's look at several dimensions of intuitive knowledge. One way to understand intuitive knowledge is to compare it with rationally determined or logical knowledge. Ornstein says:

The logical mode of knowledge operates sequentially, arriving at truth inferentially, proceeding logically from one element to another. Intuition operates simultaneously, is concerned with the sets of relations among elements, which receive their meaning from the overall holistic context. Reason, then, primarily involves an analysis of discrete elements, inferentially (sequentially) linked; intuition involves a simultaneous perception of the whole. . . . It is not the individual, discrete objects, elements, or even ideas which are themselves changed in the shift from a logical mode of consciousness to an intuitive one. Rather, it is the relationship between the elements which change, and the interpretation of a given bit of sensory data may be different depending on the context.[6]

Bruyn personalizes his definition of intuition. He says that intuition

. . . is that knowledge which is derived from the feelings, sentiments, and manifest human spirit which has acquired some measure of independence from the senses and the logical powers of man. As we conceive it, intuition is the capacity to apprehend personal meanings which inhere in a social context. *It is a human capacity which, like logic or sense, can be disciplined, and a set of procedures may be developed around it for purposes of gaining knowledgeable access to this portion of man's nature.*[7]

A word often used to describe intuitive knowledge is "insight." Insight can take the form of a new idea, a new relationship among seemingly disparate objects, a solution to a problem, a consciousness of clarity in something that before was vague and unclear. An insight may be a new way of putting together old ideas. It may be a realization of a personal problem or difficulty that results from a consciousness-raising experience. As Rollo May points out, "insights emerge not chiefly because they are 'rationally true' or even helpful, but

---

[6]Ibid., p.. 46–47.

[7]Severyn T. Bruyn, *The Human Perspective in Sociology*, Prentice-Hall, Englewood Cliffs, N.J., 1966, p. 167.

because they have a certain form, the form that is beautiful because it completes an incomplete Gestalt."[8]

Guidelines for Intuitive Research

Rational or logical thought proceeds step by step through a process such as the problem-solving approach suggested by John Dewey and emulated by many of those who write books on research methods in the social sciences.[9]

As there are generally accepted approaches for rational or logical thought and research, there are also approaches for intuitive thought and research. But we must be careful about comparing a rational approach with an intuitive approach. Rational research can be planned in sequential steps. In one sense, intuition can only be prepared for and awaited.

For example, we cannot decide to have insights; we may or may not obtain insights (intuitive knowledge) from following a preplanned thought process. An insight may not occur to us when we are working on a given piece of research. Instead, the insight may come when we are relaxing, playing tennis, carrying out the garbage, or dreaming.

What, then, are some of the conditions that encourage the development of intuitive knowledge?

Bruner[10] suggests several conditions that are necessary if intuitive knowledge is to emerge. We'll look briefly at four of them, including related reflections from Rollo May's work.

Detachment and Commitment For intuition to operate according to Bruner, people must detach themselves from the obvious ways of thinking about a problem or situation. At the same time, however, they must maintain an attitude of deep caring and motivation to find an answer. And he emphasizes that the individual must be deeply committed to this task.

Most writers on creative thought or approaches to tapping intuitive

---

[8]Rollo May, *The Courage to Create*, Norton, New York, 1975, p. 68.

[9]See the following as examples:

John Dewey, *How We Think*, Regnery, Chicago, 1933.

David J. Fox, *The Research Process in Education*, Holt, New York, 1969.

Fred N. Kerlinger, *Foundations of Behavioral Research*, Holt, New York, 1964.

Julian L. Simon, *Basic Methods in Social Science*, Random House, New York, 1969.

Deobold B. Van Dalen, *Understanding Educational Research: An Introduction*, 3d ed., McGraw-Hill, New York, 1973.

[10]Jerome S. Bruner, *On Knowing: Essays for the Left Hand*, Belknap Press of Harvard University, Cambridge, 1962, pp. 23–30.

knowledge and deriving insights mention the importance of leaving the situation for a time. This means literally doing something else. If there is anything mysterious about intuitive knowledge, it is this dimension. At this point, the unconscious works to wrestle with the input that we have provided.

It's also important to point out that the insights don't come hit or miss. There can be no insight if there hasn't been input and if there hasn't been careful and deep involvement with the situation or problem. Insights

> *may indeed occur at times of relaxation . . . or at other times when we alternate play with work. But what is entirely clear is that they pertain to those areas in which the person consciously has worked laboriously and with dedication . . . we cannot will to have insights. We cannot will creativity. But we can will to give ourselves to encounter with intensity of dedication and commitment. The deeper aspects of awareness are activated to the extent that the person is committed to the encounter.*[11]

Passion and Decorum   According to Bruner, people engaging in intuitive research must not only be committed to exploring a problem but also deeply involved in the process. They must become completely caught up in the activity. They become emotionally involved, excited about what they are doing. May talks about the intensity of the encounter. "Absorption, being caught up in, wholly involved, and so on, are used commonly to describe the state of the artist or scientist when creating or even the child at play. By whatever name one calls it, genuine creativity is characterized by an intensity of awareness, a heightened consciousness.[12]

The encounter of the person with the situation or the problem is often so intense that the person is literally taken over by it. Novelists know the meaning of this well. They often spend weeks developing the characters for their books, describing them physically, working out their motivations, defining their problems of living, and so on. And when the novelist begins writing, he or she often reports that the book is writing itself because the characters have taken over. The novelist has become the mechanism that enables the characters to play out their roles.

Another way of describing the intensity of the encounter is to say that we have internalized the situation. The situation has become a part of us—it is no longer *out there* but rather with us and in us; we cannot avoid dealing with it. It has grasped us.

[11]May, op. cit. p. 46.
[12]Ibid., p. 44.

But this intensity of encounter, this passion, must be accompanied by what Bruner calls decorum. People may be intensely involved in what they do, but they must also recognize the importance of form, structure, definitions of words, and ways of making sense of their excitement. Both passion and decorum must exist together. Passion releases and energizes. Decorum brings order and structure.

To summarize, approaches to intuitive knowledge can be learned. Everyone has the potential for discovering intuitive knowledge, both the researcher and the researched. The approach to intuitive knowledge is not mystical, although, as May suggested, we cannot *will* to have insights. But we can carefully prepare an environment in which intuition can occur. That is what the guidelines are designed to provide.

COMBINING RATIONAL–EMPIRICAL WITH INTUITIVE RESEARCH APPROACHES

Although it is quite evident that rational–empirical knowledge and intuitive knowledge are quite different from each other, is it not possible to consider combining research approaches to provide for both types of knowledge? If we subscribe to a holistic view of continuing education and the adult learner, then doesn't it follow that we must be concerned with a holistic view of knowledge?

As Ornstein says, "The piecemeal and analytic mode of organizing thought and action, which has been long ingrained and continually triumphed in the particular cultural evolution and material 'ascent' of Western society, needs supplantation by a more complete, holistic perspective."[13]

In fact, we do have some beginnings in continuing education research of approaches that attempt to tie together the intuitive with the rational–empirical. For instance, there is a group of researchers, many of them working in international settings, who advocate what they call participatory research. They draw many of their ideas from the work of Mead, Blumer, Glaser and Strauss, Filstead, and Freire.[14]

Hall has enumerated guidelines that many of these researchers follow:

1.   A research process can be of immediate and direct benefit to a

---

[13]Ornstein, op. cit., pp. 35–36.

[14]Anselm Strauss (ed.), *The Social Psychology of George Herbert Mead*, Phoenix Books, The University of Chicago Press, Chicago, 1956; Herbert Blumer, *Symbolic Interactionism*, Prentice-Hall, Englewood Cliffs, N.J., 1969; G. B. Glaser and A. L. Strauss, *The Discovery of Grounded Theory*, Aldine, Chicago, 1967; W. J. Filstead, *Qualitative Methodology*, Markham, Chicago, 1970; Paulo Freire, *Pedagogy of the Oppressed*, Herder and Herder, New York, 1971.

community (as opposed to serving merely as the basis for an academic paper or obscure policy analysis).

2. *A research process should involve the community or population in the entire research project from the formulation of the problem to the discussion of how to seek solutions and the interpretations of the findings.*

3. *The research process should be seen as part of a total educational experience which serves to establish community needs, and increases awareness and commitment within the community.*

4. *The research process should be viewed as a dialectic process, a dialogue over time and not as a static picture from one point in time.*

5. *The object of the research process, like the object of the educational process, should be the liberation of human creative potential and the mobilization of human resources for the solution of social problems.*

6. *A research process has ideological implication. A research process which allows for popular involvement and increased capacities or analysis may also make new political actions possible.*[15]

In terms of the process to be followed, Hall suggests:

The research process should be based on a system of discussion, investigation and analysis in which the researched are as much a part of the process as the researcher. Theories are neither developed beforehand to be tested nor drawn by the researcher from his or her involvement with reality. Reality is described by the process through which a community develops its own theories and solutions about itself.[16]

Of course, this approach to research is certainly not without its critics. Setting aside the obvious criticism that might be expected from people who adhere to rigidly fixed definitions of scientific research, the approach described here can be criticized as not adding to a body of knowledge. This research seems to imply that each situation is unique and different from every other. If we must start every research anew without any reliance on an existing body of knowledge—indeed this approach actually seems to deny an existing body of knowledge—how will a field of continuing education ever be developed? Of course, it could be argued that it is not important to develop a field of

[15]Budd L. Hall, *Creating Knowledge: Breaking the Monopoly*, International Council for Adult Education, Toronto (no date), pp. 9–13.

[16]Ibid., p. 11.

continuing education with its accompanying body of knowledge. But as long as we place emphasis on preparing people who will seek professional positions within the field of continuing education, it is important that we constantly strive to develop such a body of knowledge. But is it not possible to develop a body of knowledge and at the same time follow the guidelines and research approaches suggested by the participation researchers?

Bruyn suggests a slightly different approach, perhaps with more emphasis on objective research, in what he describes as participant-observer research.

> *The participant observer initially seeks to locate particular meanings which people share through communications. He is immediately concerned with whether what he identifies and describes as existent meanings really exist. Like the empiricist, the participant observer's accuracy of identification of what is really there with what he defines as being there has much to do with the validity of his work. . . . [he] is ultimately concerned with the accurate description of the total configuration of meanings existing within his universe of study. . . .*[17]

Bruyn, in contrast to the participation researchers, says the researcher must define the problem to be researched before going into the field. Second, Bruyn says the literature dealing with the subject should be studied, the design for the research should be worked out, and clearance should be obtained for "entering into the field situation as a natural part of the social setting."[18]

In the clearance phase, the researcher attempts to establish a human relationship with those studied; he or she allows the subjects to judge whether the researcher (observer's) role will be compatible with their standards.

Bruyn then describes a procedure for recording, assembling, classifying, and interpreting data.

> *The two methodologies—traditional empiricism and participant observation—may be roughly considered to be the two ways in which the social scientist establishes adequacy at objective and subjective levels respectively. . . . the participant observer cannot ignore the problem of maintaining objectivity in his reports and investigations even though he seeks to make adequate subjective descriptions . . . he must record and interpret subjective meanings accurately within an objective framework.*[19]

[17]Bruyn, op. cit. pp. 200–201.
[18]Ibid., p. 202.
[19]Ibid., p. 205.

Leon McKenzie, in an attempt to "discover" some of the intuitive knowledge to be found in fictional literature, has developed an interesting approach which he calls literary research. The approach includes careful observation, comparative analysis, and the formulation of generalizations. McKenzie's interest has been in adult development. When he goes to a novel with the intention of obtaining intuitive knowledge about adult human development, he asks such questions as:

When precisely in the story did the character emerge from childhood? What events or situational forces influenced the growth of the character toward muturity? What was the learning style of the character early in his life as compared with later in his life? What events or situational forces contributed to a change of learning style? Can the character's growth be charted according to well-defined stages? What are these stages? [20]

McKenzie, who is well aware of the knowledge in the field of human development from rational–empirical sources, is seeking to compare and combine this knowledge with that which comes from an intuitive process—the process the artist (novelist) uses in creating new knowledge. McKenzie's process, then, focuses on the artist as a source of knowledge which can be added to the store of rational–empirical knowledge. McKenzie's purpose and hope is that such research will at least confirm some of the findings of rational–empirical research. But there is also the possibility that he may discover some new insights, presented by novelists, that may allow the total research (in this case in human development) to move ahead or away from the point at which the rational–empirical researchers are now.

SUMMARY

Given the existing contradictions between the commonly accepted programming approaches in continuing education and the predominant research approach, several guidelines were suggested for developing new approaches to research in continuing education:

1. Knowledge does not exist apart from values.
2. Researchers should examine their research in light of their assumptions and should make these assumptions explicit.

[20]Leon McKenzie, "Analysis of Bildungsroman Literature as a Research Modality in Adult Education: An Inquiry," *Adult Education*, vol. 25, no. 4, pp. 209–215, 1975.

3. Research in continuing education should further the purposes of the field of continuing education.
4. Research in continuing education should involve the researched (the adult learner) as a subject in the process, not as an object to be studied from a distance.
5. Research in continuing education should be of assistance to those researched and at the same time have the potential for adding to a body of knowledge.
6. The practice of continuing education, and continuing education research should always be linked.
7. *Research in continuing education should view knowledge broadly.*

It was emphasized that researchers in continuing education should attempt to combine rational–empirical with intuitive research approaches. Some attention was given to describing intuitive knowledge and comparing it with rational–empirical knowledge.

Drawing primarily on the work of May and Bruner, several guidelines for conducting intuitive research were discussed.

Finally, several examples of attempts to combine rational–empirical with intuitive research approaches were presented.

SUGGESTED READINGS

Chamberlin, J. Gordon: *Toward a Phenomenology of Education*, Westminster, Philadelphia, 1969.

Bono, Edward de: *Lateral Thinking*, Harper & Row, New York, 1970.

Griffith, William S., Malcolm S. Knowles, Paul H. Sheats, and Cyril O. Houle: "Research in Adult Education: Perspectives and New Directions," *Adult Leadership*, vol. 20, no. 8, February 1972.

Kuhn, Thomas S.: *The Structure of Scientific Revolutions,* The University of Chicago Press, Chicago, 1962.

Long, Huey B., and Stephen K. Agyekum: "Adult Education 1964–1973: Reflections of a Changing Discipline," *Adult Education*, vol. 24, no. 2, pp. 99–120, 1974.

Ohliger, John, and John Niemi: "Annotated and Quotational Bibliography on Participatory Research," *Convergence*, vol. 8, no. 2, pp. 82–87, 1975.

Phillips, Derek L.: *Knowledge from What*, Rand McNally, Chicago, 1971.

Rist, Ray C.: *On Qualitative Research*, College of Human Ecology, Cornell University, Ithaca, N.Y., 1978 (a bibliography).

Royce, Joseph R.: *The Encapsulated Man*, Van Nostrand, Princeton, N.J., 1964.

Wann, T. W. (ed.): *Behaviorism and Phenomenology*, The University of Chicago Press, Chicago, 1964.

INDEX

INDEX